Turkey and the Middle East

CHATHAM HOUSE PAPERS

A Middle East Programme Publication
Programme Director: Philip Robins

The Royal Institute of International Affairs, at Chatham House in London, has provided an impartial forum for discussion and debate on current international issues for some 70 years. Its resident research fellows, specialized information resources, and range of publications, conferences, and meetings span the fields of international politics, economics, and security. The Institute is independent of government.

Chatham House Papers are short monographs on current policy problems which have been commissioned by the RIIA. In preparing the papers, authors are advised by a study group of experts convened by the RIIA, and publication of a paper indicates that the Institute regards it as an authoritative contribution to the public debate. The Institute does not, however, hold opinions of its own; the views expressed in this publication are the responsibility of the author.

CHATHAM HOUSE PAPERS

Turkey and the Middle East

Philip Robins

The Royal Institute of International Affairs

Pinter Publishers
London

© Royal Institute of International Affairs, 1991

First published in Great Britain in 1991 by
Pinter Publishers Limited
25 Floral Street, London WC2E 9DS

British Library Cataloguing in Publication Data

A CIP catalogue record of this book is available from the British Library

ISBN 0-86187-199-5 (Paperback)
0-86187-198-7 (Hardback)

Reproduced from copy supplied by
Koinonia Limited
Printed and bound in Great Britain by
Biddles Ltd

CONTENTS

Contents

For Helen

ACKNOWLEDGMENTS

Many people have given advice and insight in the preparation of this study. The confidential basis on which discussions and interviews took place prohibit the mentioning of their names. I would, however, like to single out Professor William Wallace, Mina Toksoz, Andrew Mango, Angela Gillan and Helen Robins, all of whom read drafts of the text and gave valuable comments. Needless to say I accept full responsibility for the analysis contained within this book.

I must also thank my colleagues on the Middle East Programme for their stimulating company and expertise. Sir John Moberly continues to show a tireless commitment to the fortunes of the programme; his measured advice and experience has been of great benefit to me both as author and as programme head. Jill Kalawoun, the programme assistant, capably administered the project, as well as making a valued contribution at the research level. Margaret May patiently and diligently handled the publications side of the operation.

Finally I would like to thank the two sponsors of the project, the National Institute for Research Advancement in Tokyo and the Ford Foundation in New York. I greatly appreciate their commitment to a study, the topicality of which came to the surface some time after they had agreed to its funding.

March 1991   P.R.

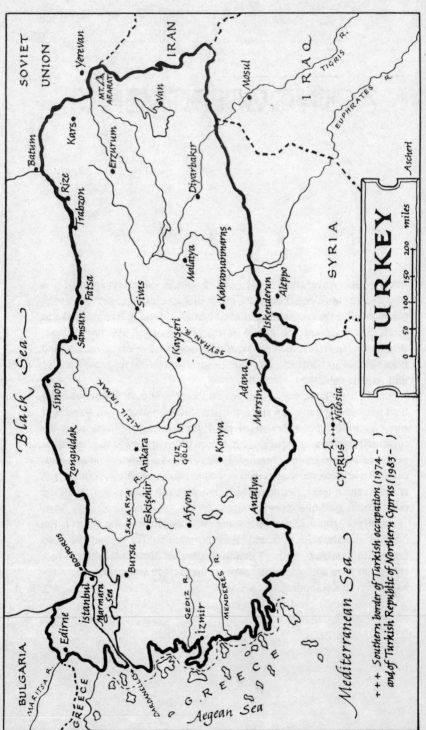

++ Southern border of Turkish occupation (1974–)
and of Turkish Republic of Northern Cyprus (1983–)

1

INTRODUCTION

There has been a noticeable lack of scholarly research on Turkey. In view of its sizeable population and landmass, and given its continuing importance over four decades as both a member of the Nato alliance and a 'frontline' state with the USSR, this may seem surprising. But Turkey does not fit into any neat geographical or linguistic categories, and so is consistently and unjustifiably ignored by Europeanists, Sovietologists and Arabists alike.

Studies of Turkey from an international relations perspective put Turkish-speaking scholars, both foreign and Anatolian, at an immediate disadvantage because of the narrowness of their expertise. They lack the broader inter-state perspective of the area studies specialist. Turkish-speaking academics and international think-tanks alike tend to tread the predictable ground of the Cyprus problem, Greece, the Soviet threat and, more recently, membership of the European Community. Turkey's relations with the Middle East (as, indeed, with the Balkans) are consistently ignored. Even in Turkey itself the subject is largely neglected, partly because resources are not available within the country and partly because there is little interest among Turkish academics. Both reasons are indicative of the Kemalist view of Turkey's foreign policy priorities, and the values of the Kemalist cadres inside the republic. And both go some way towards explaining the lack of understanding which Turkey periodically displays for its Middle Eastern neighbours, and the policy problems which result.

This study arose from a desire to bridge the gap in the existing literature. More specifically, it emerged from a number of questions

1

which were asked about Turkey's interests and policies in the context of earlier work on the Iran–Iraq war. The ceasefire in August 1988 did not halt such questions, as the issues of water, the Kurds and the spread of Islamism have all served to bind Turkey more firmly into the Middle East sub-system of states. The Gulf crisis arising from the Iraqi invasion of Kuwait in 1990 again underlined Turkey's important role in the area. And if the changes taking place across Europe and in the Soviet Union do not reorient Turkey more firmly towards the East, a resurgence of Gulf prosperity based upon a sustained upswing in the oil market, whenever that should take place, certainly will.

This study starts by considering how certain 'Middle East phenomena' affect domestic Turkish politics and society. Domestic issues are linked with foreign relations to emphasize the inextricability of Turkey's involvement with the Middle East and the wider Islamic community. These wider themes are developed in later chapters. Of course, to limit one's focus solely to the Middle East is untenable and would be as mistaken as looking simply at Turkey's relations with, say, Europe. Turkey is, in the words of one diplomat, 'a bundle of linkages'. Policy decisions in one geographical direction have immediate implications in other directions. Although this is a truism of most states today, it is quite simply truer of Turkey. However, Turkey's place in the international order falls outside the scope of this book, which aims to counter the common assumption that its relations with the Middle East are unimportant.

2

TURKEY'S UNCERTAIN IDENTITY

The absence of analytical writings on Turkey means that a study of its relations with the Middle East cannot begin by assuming that it is a known quantity. A glance at the map shows why. Turkey lies in Asia, and yet its best-known part and business capital lie in the European landmass. It is a Mediterranean state, yet its Black Sea shores are just as long. Turkey does not fit into any of the neat geographical categories which Western scholars have formulated to organize a spatially messy world. The geographical facts indicate wider uncertainties about the placing and role of the country.

A sense of confusion about Turkey is not, however, confined to the external perspective. There appears to be some considerable doubt even among Turks of similar socio-economic background as to the exact nature of the country and its people, and how this should manifest itself in the external relations of the state. The debate and equivocation over membership of the European Community perhaps best illustrates this uncertainty of identity within the republic.

Identity of the people
The end of World War I left the disparate people of Anatolia as broken and as dispirited as the Ottoman state of which they were subjects. There was every prospect of Asia Minor being parcelled up between the victorious allies. The peace talks promised little to the Turkish people apart from a fragile and inconsequential state based on 'a few provinces in Anatolia ... [with] only a single outlet to the Aegean'.[1]

3

This precarious state of affairs was retrieved by the single-minded determination of a group of nationalist army officers under the leadership of Mustafa Kemal Atatürk. The Kemalists were first successful in establishing a state based on the whole of Anatolia. They then relentlessly pursued the consolidation of the state and the achievement of national sovereignty, and, led principally by Atatürk himself, went on to define the state's norms and values.

The fact that Atatürk felt the need to define a new ideology[2] for the state, and was apparently so successful in doing so, illustrates the ideological vacuum within which he was working. The imperial pan-Islamism of the Ottoman Empire, in which the Turks as an ethno-linguistic group were in a minority, had collapsed with the Empire. The three main competing currents left were the Anatolianism to which Atatürk broadly subscribed, Turanism or pan-Turkism, and a post-imperial pan-Islamism. But these movements were not widely assimilated within society, especially among the vast majority of the rural population. The range of Atatürk's reforms and the fact that he was able to brush aside opposition to them indicate the difficulty which his critics had in mobilizing the population. Ultimately, this suggests the incoherence and lack of consensus among the majority of the population, as well as their parochial, rather than national, preoccupations.

From the moment he came to power until his death in 1938, Atatürk set himself the task of defining the nature of the Turkish people, and, by extension, that of the Turkish state. He had a strong vision of what the values and norms of that state should be: it should be independent, modern, industrialized, Europe-oriented, secular, Turkish and based almost exclusively on the territory of Anatolia. In many ways these elements were mutually reinforcing. Turkey had to give up any idea of an empire in the Middle East if it was to be firmly oriented on Anatolia and convincingly secular, which in turn were prerequisites of a European identity. Consequently, the ideal citizen of Turkey would be a resident of Anatolia, nationalist, European in outlook, secular and, most important of all, would feel himself to be a Turk.

By the time of his death, Atatürk appeared to have succeeded in his aims. The Turkish state was certainly well established and accepted as a member of the international order. It was definitely independent, had renounced its former imperial territories and was formally secular. Atatürk also seemed to have been successful in creating his new Turkish citizen. His domination of Turkey during this period, through force of personality on the one hand and authoritarian political structures on the other, certainly helped create this illusion. A torrent of social and cultural legislation had changed the outward appearance of Turks, both figuratively and literally. Aspects of oriental dress were proscribed. The Latin alphabet replaced its Arabic counterpart. Outward expression of religious devotion was greatly discouraged. Most importantly, Atatürk emphasized the centrality of Turkish identity, regardless of the origins of its people. Proclaiming oneself a Turk thus became a badge of pride and the key to full membership of the state, rather than the social stigma it had been under the Ottomans.[3]

It is now more than 50 years since the death of Atatürk, and 40 years since his right-hand man, İsmet İnönü, relinquised power. Since then Turkey has edged away from austere and authoritarian politics towards greater political participation and pluralism. Yet the setting aside of strictly regulated and limiting political structures has also helped to undermine the old certainties of self-image. More and more of the limitations and contradictions of the Turkish identity, as defined by the Kemalists, are coming to the fore. Most pronounced, as Turkey moves into the 1990s, are the related issues of ethnicity, nationhood and the territorial state on the one hand and the question of religion and secularity on the other.

As already noted, the notion of Turkism was fundamental to the forging of a new identity for the state of Turkey. The emphasis on a Turkish identity, regardless of ethnic background, was initially very valuable in opposing the creation of other states which would have broken the spatial cohesion of Anatolia. This threat came principally from plans to establish an Armenian state and a Kurdish state after World War I. Once Armenian and Kurdish national aspirations had been thwarted these ethnic groups were unlikely to accept a Turkish identity or to be enthusiastic members of a Turkish state. They were unlikely to identify with Atatürk's famous maxim, 'Happy is the one who calls himself a Turk.' Turkish identity was therefore the common denominator of only those people who could be expected to support the creation of a state based on the whole of Anatolia. The constant emphasis placed on Turkism represented an attempt to gloss over barely hidden ethnic cleavages that could exert a fragmentary effect on the modern Turkish state.

The problematic nature of this heterogeneity is clear from the sensitivity with which it is treated in official circles. The 1961 constitution circumvented the problem of ethnic division simply by legislating that every citizen of the Turkish state was a Turk.[4] Such euphemisms as

'Mountain Turks' and, more recently, 'eastern compatriots' were coined to describe the Kurds.[5] While it is becoming easier to refer to the existence of Kurds in Turkey there is still no official acknowledgment that they are culturally or even ethnically distinct from the Turks.[6] Separate cultural and – until recently – linguistic rights have been formally denied, more out of the insecurity than the perversity of the majority.

The geographical concentration of much of the Kurdish population, however, draws attention to them as a discrete group. In policy terms, the existence of this community is difficult to ignore. Indeed, Kurds are a majority in eight southeastern provinces of Turkey adjacent to the borders of Iraq and Iran. The sensitivity of the minorities issue is amply illustrated by the uncertainty surrounding the size of the Kurdish population in Turkey, although this is also in part caused by the bilingualism of many Kurds.[7] Estimates differ as to the proportion of Kurds in Turkey, ranging from the official 7.1 per cent[8] to the more reasonable 17 or 18 per cent,[9] and as high as 24 per cent according to Kurdish sources. With the population of Turkey estimated to be some 57 million in 1990, the Kurdish component could be as low as 4.5 million or as high as 13.2 million, though a more plausible figure would be around 10 million.

Though the Kurds are by far the largest ethnic minority in Anatolia, others are significant. Turkey contains a small but important Arab minority. In the 1965 census respondents whose mother tongue was Arabic represented 1.2 per cent of the total population. Given the linguistic Turkification of the non-Turkic population and their reluctance to respond to a survey conducted by the Turkish state, one may assume that the Arab population is actually greater. Again, the geographical distribution of the Arabs adds to their importance. Over 40 per cent of the Arabic speakers are located near the Syrian border in Hatay, a province which is still claimed by Syria (see Chapter 3).

The ethnic question cannot be confined to the situation inside the Turkish state. Just as not all the citizens of Turkey are Turks, so not all Turks are located inside the Turkish state. The Turkish nation and the Turkish state are far from co-terminous. Ethnic Turks are to be found to the west of Turkey, in Bulgaria, Yugoslavia, Greece and Cyprus. More importantly, numerically at least, large numbers of Turks are located to the east, both in Arab countries such as Iraq and in the southern Soviet republics. After all, pan-Turkism did originally grow up at the beginning of the century among the Turkic minority of the Russian Empire.

In the recent past, however, the Turkish state has been rather more preoccupied with the plight of its cousins to the west. This was a result of the unrest in Cyprus in the 1960s followed by the occupation of the north of the island by Turkey in 1974, the periodic frictions surrounding the Turks in Western Thrace, and the attempted forced assimilation of the Turkish minority in Bulgaria. The possible breakdown of the Soviet state and the greater opportunity to build cultural and economic ties with the Turks to the east may help to reorient the direction of Turkey-centric pan-Turkism. Ultimately, Central Asia is potentially of even greater interest to the Turks of Turkey because of the perception shared by many that this is their ancestral home.

Atatürk's mission was not just to instil pride in a Turkish identity, but also to undermine Islam as a force within the politics and society of the new Turkish republic. He set about the task with single-mindedness and vigour. He attacked Islamization in three ways. First, he suppressed those institutions and organizations which existed to promote the domination of Islam over all aspects of life. To this end, Islamic schools were closed down and religious orders outlawed. Second, he replaced formal signs and symbols of an Islamic or oriental nature with those of a Christian or European nature. Among a host of measures, the weekend holiday was moved from the Islamic holy day of Friday to the Christian Sunday, and the Gregorian calendar replaced the lunar calendar of Islam. Third, the Turkish legal system was changed from being predicated on Islam to the Swiss civil code.

Atatürk did not seek the eradication of the Muslim faith, though he might privately have wished that the Turks were Christian. He made no attempt to close mosques, for example, although civil servants were discouraged from attending them. Atatürk was a politician as well as a soldier. He had a clear grasp of what was politically possible within the new Turkish state. He appreciated that in a highly rural and socially conservative country closing mosques was not a credible option, and that the complete abolition of religion was not possible. He therefore sought to harness and sublimate religion beneath the secular requirements of the state. Religion was banished from the public to the personal domain, and predominantly from the urban to the rural context. At times, however, when it was more productive, Atatürk was willing to incorporate certain aspects of religion into public life. For instance, the two major Islamic festivals were incorporated into the public holidays of the republic, alongside anniversaries of the national movement. Thus Atatürk was willing to permit 'a measure of synthesis',[10] a step perhaps more easily explained as that of a leader making the best of an unsatisfactory situation, rather than of a man who believed in a new partnership between religion and society. One may assume that to Atatürk, who had no personal faith, Islam was repugnant as a manifestation of oriental mysticism which offended the rigour of European rationalism.

There was a second, utilitarian, reason for Atatürk to relegate Islam to the level of a private faith, namely the potential divisiveness of the religious question within Turkey. It is not only in the realm of ethnicity that there is an important minority within Turkish society. In the Alevis there exists a religious minority more closely akin to Shi'ism than the majority Sunni faith in Turkey, in addition to a variety of dervish or Sufi orders which combine elements of pre-Islamic paganism with a more mystical interpretation of Sunni Islam.

The controversy surrounding the Alevis is replicated by disputes over their profile in the population. Some Alevi sources claim that they represent up to 40 per cent of the Turkish population,[11] a figure generally rejected by scholars. A more widely accepted proportion would be between 15 and 20 per cent,[12] with the latter figure, amounting to some 11.5 million at the present population level, the most frequently cited. There are no official figures for the size of the population because the Alevis are not legally recognized, their rites having been banned since Atatürk's 1925 legislation against the *tarikat*, or religious orders. Here, as with the Kurds, the Turkish government has dealt with a potentially divisive minority simply by defining it out of existence.

The denial of the existence of the Alevis is principally due to the continuing antipathy towards them from the mainstream Sunni population in Turkey. To religious Sunnis, the 'Alevis are considered to be worse than infidels, morally degenerate, and to be avoided at all costs'.[13] Periodic massacres of Alevis have been recorded between the sixteenth century and the late 1970s, when the Alevis began increasingly to identify themselves as a group. The state outlawed an Alevi political party organized around this time. The hostility of the Sunni population has tended to drive the politically active Alevis in the direction of secularism and leftism, which are increasingly fused with what is effectively a national self-awareness. One of the most extreme groups is the *Kizil Yol* (Red Path), based in Germany, which advocates the founding of Alevistan, or a nation of Alevis. It takes as its model the attempt by Kurdish separatists to establish a Kurdish state.[14]

The aims of *Kizil Yol* would probably not be supported by most of the Alevis in Turkey, for several reasons. First, the community continues to be less well organized, its group consciousness still limited to local areas. Moreover, in the past the Alevis have tended to deal with their own persecution not by self-assertion but through the practice of *taqqiya*, a tactical public disavowal of their faith. Second, the Alevis are a confessional rather than an ethnic group. It remains to be seen whether this can provide a sound bedrock for a national-style movement; comparisons with the Kurds are at least premature and probably misleading. Third, the Alevis are far from being a homogeneous group, instead containing ethnic and linguistic cleavages. The four different language groups found among them are Turkish, Arabic, Zaza and Kurmanci, the latter two being Persian- and Kurdish-related language systems.[15]

The dervish orders are numerous and varied, and stretch back many centuries in Anatolia, where they have tended to prosper in the central, rural areas. On a spiritual plane, the orders have traditionally satisfied the popular wish for a more mystical religious experience. They have also fulfilled social and economic functions, which explains their resilience in the face of persecution, as well as the loyalty of their followers. The orders continue to flourish and have become something of a free-masonry. The larger, better-known orders, such as the Nakş ibendi and the Nurcu, have networks throughout the country, and can count on the support of tens of thousands of adherents. The very nature of the organizations brings them into competition with the state, while their emotional religiosity makes them almost the antithesis of the sterile rationality of Kemalism.

Until the 1970s the Turkish state proved capable of managing these centrifugal forces, but since then it has increasingly appeared to founder. It has struggled to preserve the essential secularity of the state against a growing personal piety and a greater interest in Islam as a political force. It has struggled to maintain the internal security of the state, especially in the Kurdish southeast. It may be on the verge of having to grapple with a rejuvenated pan-Turkism, which is oriented towards the geographical origins of the Turkish people of Anatolia. Though the secularity and territoriality of the state may ultimately win through, the struggle is being waged against a backdrop of increasing uncertainty and confusion as to the identity of the Turkish people and the basis of the state of Turkey.

Identity of the state

During the heyday of the Ottoman Empire, Istanbul and the Turkish heartland were located in the middle of a politically important region, and formed the power centre of one of the major international actors of the day. To the west lay the empire's European provinces; to the south and east was its Middle Eastern area. The importance of the Ottoman Empire and its domains in Europe and the Middle East meant that, like Rome and Byzantium before it, it defied geography, both physically and politically.

The demise of empires and the emergence of the nation-state has meant that Turkey has now succumbed to its geography. Anatolia is no longer at the heart of a state, it *is* the state. True, this has raised the importance of the Anatolian heartland which, though at the physical centre of the Ottoman Empire, was never considered its essence. However, it has also resulted in the inevitable marginalization of that state in international terms. For despite its vast landmass, covering an area of some 770,760 square kilometres, Turkey is located on the periphery of three great political continents: Europe, the Middle East and the Russian core of the Soviet Union. Though too large and important to be ignored by any of these three, by the same token Turkey is doomed to exclusion from any central role in their affairs.

In many respects the Kemalist ideology of the Turkish state contributed to this political marginalization. Atatürk set great store on the cohesion of the Turkish people, and on their differences from the peoples of adjacent states. This philosophy was reflected in Turkish diplomacy. Turkey was stoically isolated in the 1920s. The economic policy of the new state was grimly autarkic, despite Atatürk's rhetorical pledge to make Turkey a European power. Of course, it could not and did not exist divorced from developments elsewhere in the world. Atatürk cultivated good relations with the Soviet Union in the 1920s. He took Turkey into a major alliance, the Balkan Pact, in 1934. Nevertheless, from the conclusion of the Lausanne Treaty in 1923 to the Anglo-Franco-Turkish Treaty of 19 October 1939 Turkey assiduously guarded its non-aligned status. Even having admitted the need for 'powerful friends', it managed to remain directly uninvolved in World War II.[16]

Atatürk's firm policy of retrenchment to a Turkish core was the foundation of his philosophy. The political style of the day provided the vehicle for the articulation of this neo-nationalism. His emphasis on the links between the Anatolian Turks and the heroic Hittites of antiquity bordered on the mystical. A product of Messianic chauvinism, such ideas have persevered in the strongholds of Kemalism, such as the army, long after the demise of comparable movements in Germany and Italy.

The residue of this mystical self-belief and the frigid isolationism which it spawned is instilled in Turkey's diplomacy today. The Turkish approach to international relations is underpinned by a brooding suspicion of all states, friend and foe alike. And the grudging legalism of the early years of the republic are still found near the surface of Turkish diplomacy.

The geographical marginality of Turkey, together with the strong strain of isolationism engrained during the Kemalist reign, has been further crystallized by the suspicions of Turkey's neighbours. A brief look at its relations with its immediate neighbours will highlight how awkwardly modern Turkey manages its geographical context. Iran, as a former imperial state and regional power of broadly similar size, still sees Turkey as a potential competitor for power and influence in the Middle East region. The Arab view of Turkey is all the more pejorative, growing as it does out of a deep sense of inferiority and bitterness at its past centuries of subjugation to the Ottoman core. For many of the regimes in the Islamic world whose legitimacy rests on their commitment to uphold-ing the faith, such as Saudi Arabia, the laicism of Turkey has been perceived as at best an object of suspicion, at worst an alternative model of government capable of subverting the power of traditional regimes.

Turkey's uneasy relations are not confined to the Middle East. To the west, relations with Greece soured once again in 1990, with the furore in Turkey over the treatment of the Turks in Western Thrace. The relation-ship has thus returned to the brooding animosity and suspicion which has pervaded bilateral ties for most of this century. The brief flicker of hope provided by the Davos reconciliation in January 1988 has been all but extinguished. The Cyprus problem, and in particular both Turkey's occupation of the north of the island and its lone support for the inde-pendent state declared by the Turkish Cypriots, continues to be a focus of resentment for Greeks in Cyprus and Greece and for Hellenophiles around the world.

Elsewhere in the Balkans, Turkey experienced great tensions with the Bulgarian regime over Todor Zhivkov's Bulgarianization policy. In sum-mer 1989 matters came to a head, with large numbers of Turkic Bul-garians fleeing across the border. Zhivkov was ousted from power soon after, and his policies towards the Turkish minority were rescinded, provoking a sizeable backlash within the non-Turkic Bulgarian majority. This indicated a deep sense of anxiety on the part of Bulgarians about the country's growing Turkish minority. In view of the enduring popularity of the anti-Turkic legislation and the primordial nature of the intercommunal suspicions, the thaw in Turkish–Bulgarian relations can-not be guaranteed. More generally in the Balkans, the Muslim–Christian cleavage could reappear as a major faultline, putting Turkey in a difficult

11

position. At best, the dichotomy could underpin existing ethnic problems. Tensions from either source could erupt into conflict in Bulgaria, or in Yugoslavia over the predominantly Muslim province of Kosovo; such conflict could escalate with Albanian involvement; and, as the largest Muslim power in the region, Turkey would find its relations with its Christian neighbours growing cooler were real instability to result. And the fact that many Turks are recent descendants of migrants from the Balkans adds to Turkey's difficulties in trying to dodge what many would construe as its obligations there.

Since the end of World War II Turkey has been most concerned about Soviet expansionism, which appeared directly to threaten Turkish sovereignty. Indeed, Stalin's 'grab for the Straits' was one of the chief causes of the Cold War in 1947. It was Moscow's heavy-handedness that drove Turkey into membership of Nato, and conditioned the strategic thinking of a generation of Turkish military commanders. Since then Soviet policy towards Turkey has attempted to undo the damage done by Stalin.[17] While Soviet–Turkish relations thawed in the 1960s and even warmed during the 1970s, the invasion of Afghanistan revived fears of Soviet expansionism. As a result, the Turkish establishment has been slower than most of its Nato partners to respond to Mikhail Gorbachev's 'new thinking' in foreign policy. As a regional power adjacent to a superpower, Turkey's reticence towards its powerful neighbour is understandable. The use of the Soviet armed forces against the Turkic city of Baku in Azerbaijan in January 1990 is likely to prolong it. Furthermore, when placed alongside the EC's essentially negative stance on Turkey's application for membership and the reaction in the West to the Baku intervention, there has already been a rekindling of Turkish concerns at a deepening Christian-cum-European solidarity against the Muslim peoples on the European rim.

The sense of diplomatic isolation born of Turkey's difficulties with its immediate neighbours has been further exacerbated by its uneasy relationship with its friends. Turkey's rejection by Western Europe is the most crushing example of this. The Opinion of the European Commission in December 1989 on Turkey's 1987 application for membership was couched in diplomatic language. However, the implications for Turkey were that it would not be possible to begin accession negotiations before 1993 at the earliest, and that a host of long-term economic and political problems were still to be resolved. The Turkish government endeavoured to 'put a brave face' on the Commission's Opinion,[18] and President Özal even called it positive beyond Turkey's expectations.[19] However, the

Opinion was regarded by the US, an ally of both sides, so arguably best placed to adjudicate, as a clear rebuff.[20] It was also seen, in one Muslim perspective, as the latest example of 'Turkey bashing'.[21] In private, Turkish mainstream opposition politicians confided that the opinion indicated that Turkey was unlikely ever to gain full admission to the EC.

Turkey has a mercurial relationship even with its most important ally, the United States. This results primarily from the domestic influence of the Greek and Armenian lobbies in the USA. It has been exacerbated by Ankara's inability to comprehend the anarchic pluralism of the US political system. For instance, when the Armenian Remembrance Day legislation was before Congress in February 1990, Turkey introduced a package of sanctions against the United States. Thus the Turks played into the hands of the resolution's sponsors both by drawing attention to it and by ensuring that it helped to blight bilateral relations. Given Turkish membership of Nato and the presence of joint US–Turkish military bases, it seemed a matter for both surprise and concern that in a Turkish public opinion poll in February 1990 over 30 per cent of respondents named the United States as a country unfriendly to Turkey.[22] Only Greece and Bulgaria, with 35 per cent and 32.2 per cent respectively, scored higher. Indeed, it is instructive that the state with which Turkey arguably has the best relations is Pakistan. This view appears to be held at both the elite and popular levels. In the same poll, 28.3 per cent of respondents named Pakistan as the country most friendly towards Turkey; next came the Turkish Republic of Northern Cyprus, scoring 15.3 per cent. Pakistan is similar to Turkey in being on the periphery of the Middle East, yet deeply affected by developments in that region. Moreover, it too is a regional power situated close to a superpower, the Soviet Union, which has been routinely perceived as a threat. Both states have strong armed forces. These similarities perhaps explain an extra empathy which transcends transitory politicians and governments. In addition, Turkey and Pakistan have none of the bilateral difficulties which tarnish Turkish relations with other states in the region. Most importantly, Turkey and Pakistan do not have a common border.

Turkey's response to what it perceives as this pervasive hostility has been twofold. First, it has sought entry to a variety of clubs of states to both west and east. Thus it is a member of the Council of Europe and Nato on the one hand, and the Islamic Conference Organization (ICO) on the other. In this way, and in claiming to be part of both the secular and the Islamic worlds, Turkey has sought to make the best of its foothold in two continents. Its place in both the Council of Europe and the ICO has led to repeated claims that it is 'a bridge' from one continent to another, from one culture to another. Such claims are weak and unconvincing. Turkey does, of course, provide a bridge in a literal sense between Europe and Asia, and much traffic between the two crosses the sub-continent at this point. But politically and philosophically, the claim collapses. The truth is that rather than understanding both continents and both cultures, and hence having a unique role as interpreter to both, Turkey comprehends neither adequately to fulfil this role. Its relationship with the Arabs, the Persians and the majority of the Islamic states is confused and tentative. Its relationship with the West is increasingly marked by suspicion and resentment. Moreover, divisions within Turkey, between Western-educated, urban businessmen and intellectuals, and the rural, personally pious peasants, mirror the divisions between the two continents that it straddles.

Furthermore, its membership of these organizations has not brought greater understanding of Turkey to its fellow members. Neither has it been an automatic ticket to other, more integrated clubs of states. Most obviously, Turkey's membership of Nato has not brought admission to either the Western European Union or the European Community, both of which Turkey aspires to join. Yet it has had a positive psychological effect upon the Turkish state and its elite groups. The membership that it has achieved has partially compensated for the sense of psychological isolation which would otherwise have been felt more keenly. However, even this benefit is under threat. The *de facto* rejection of Turkey by the only club really worth being in, the EC, together with the declining importance of Nato, is fast undermining the effectiveness of this strategy at a time when the membership of clubs is becoming a global fashion.

The second way in which Turkey has responded to this political isolation has been by falling back on its own resources, and seeking to become more self-reliant. This strategy has been pursued to varying degrees since the establishment of the modern state of Turkey. Much has already been said about how this was addressed in a cultural and ideological sense. The notion of self-reliance was also evident politically in the first years of the republic and during World War II. The strategy of non-alignment was abandoned only because of the real, imminent threat from the Soviet Union. Even on the issue of defence policy, Turkey has not relinquished its own ability to defend itself in favour of an overall Nato umbrella. It has maintained a large, labour-intensive, conscript army from the days of the independence war to the recent, qualitatively enhanced threat perceived from the Soviet Union.

Even over a subject as close to the hearts of today's Turkish elites as membership of the EC, Ankara has not always been unequivocal. Significantly, both Turkey and Greece concluded association agreements with the EC at the same time – under the Treaty of Ankara, signed in December 1964. Yet in the late 1970s Turkey vacillated during the Greek application to join the Community and so lost a vital opportunity to enhance its prospects of membership.

The philosophy of self-reliance also pervaded economic policy, at least until the 1980s. In the early years of the state an autarkic approach was equated with national independence. Negative experiences of free trade, both with the capitulations of the Ottoman period and as part of the Treaty of Lausanne,[23] have taken a long time to dissipate. The first decades of the republic saw the establishment of an import substitution philosophy which led to the expansion of the state bureaucracy. The State Economic Enterprises came to dominate, especially in the manufacturing sector. There has been a pronounced change of strategy over the last decade. The Turkish economy has boomed, but only at the price of spiralling debt, high inflation and growing unemployment. There are, however, still substantial areas of the economy which remain predominantly untouched by the philosophy of economic liberalization that has prevailed since the early 1980s.

A third response may emerge in the future, depending on the eventual fate of the Soviet Central Asian republics and Azerbaijan. They are overwhelmingly populated by Turkic peoples and they offer some hope of the sort of community of states based on strong common characteristics which Turkey has lacked, to its disadvantage, over the past decades. If the southern Soviet republics were to have the opportunity of independence, a Turkic commonwealth might become a possibility. Some observers believe that this would be attractive to Turkey, especially in view of its repeated isolation, perceived and actual, over many issues in the international community. The residual Soviet state, worried no doubt about the establishment of young and potentially weak states on its southern flank, could welcome a role for Turkey here. The caution and maturity of Turkey's Moscow policy in recent years will help in this respect.

Should the Soviet Union stand firmly in the way of independence for its southern republics, this too might serve Turkish interests. The Soviet state seems likely to be a looser affair in the future, with individual republics cultivating their own external economic and cultural relations. This would give the Turkic republics the ability to develop relations with

Turkey on a number of levels. Indeed, the process appears already to have begun. In January 1990 Turkey prepared a protocol for cultural and scientific cooperation with Azerbaijan, independent of the programme signed earlier between Ankara and Moscow. This was the first such agreement between Turkey and a Soviet republic.[24] At the same time the individual Turkic republics' continued membership of the Soviet Union could help Turkey fend off demands for economic assistance, which its delicate economy would not be well placed to give.

In the meantime, Turkey is left without a natural community of states of which it can feel properly a part. It does not have the Arab people's strong, fraternal trans-statal bond or the Iranian mullahs' hope of establishing a religion-based international leadership role. Though a member of the ICO, Turkey is not fully integrated. Its avowed secularism is difficult to stomach for a religion where personal faith and way of life cannot be separated.

For a variety of complex economic, political and cultural reasons the European Community, increasingly co-terminous with the European continent itself, is keen to keep Turkey at arm's length. The new independent states of Central and Eastern Europe are more likely to look to Brussels for an economic and diplomatic lead than to attempt to establish a second community in Europe. They are likely to come to reject Turkey for the same reasons as their EC counterparts, with the additional reason of wanting to supply the demand for labour in Western Europe over the next two decades. Turkey seems destined to continue to be an unwelcome outsider on the margins of both Europe and the Middle East for the foreseeable future.

3
HISTORICAL REFERENCE POINTS

The relationship between Anatolia and the Middle East has, until recently, been closely intertwined. From the sixteenth century until the end of World War I most of the Middle East, with the major exception of Iran, was part of the Ottoman Empire. Although Ottoman authority was often notional, in the major cities closest to Anatolia its influence was considerable.[1] Since the dissolution of the empire, the relationship between Turkey and the states of the Middle East has become more complex, formal and differentiated. The Muslims who populated the empire are now distinguished from each other not only by traditional parochial differences, such as kinship, economic function and the urban–rural divide, but also by cultural, linguistic-based nationalism, such as Arabism and Turkism, and by territorial nationalism in the individual Arab states.

This chapter explores the historical legacy of Turkish–Middle Eastern relations, focusing on reference points which are still highly relevant to the relationship today: the Ottoman legacy, the cases of disputed territory – Hatay/Alexandretta and Mosul – and the Baghdad Pact.

The Ottoman legacy
The Ottoman Empire was not typical of the European empires of the eighteenth and nineteenth centuries, whose underlying characteristic was that of a distinct people of the metropolitan core, motivated by a nationalist ideology, seeking the subjugation of peoples in a geographical periphery. While integration of core and periphery into one state did sometimes occur, for instance in the case of parts of the French empire, elite

17

integration was on the whole negligible. The Ottoman Empire, by contrast, was not a Turkish empire in which the ideological motivation was Turkish nationalism. In many respects rural Anatolia was as much a domain of the empire as parts of the Balkans or the Middle East. The chief motivating ideology of the state was Islam, especially as the profile of the empire in Christian Europe receded. Moreover, rather like the Roman empire, the Ottoman Empire believed much more in assimilating its territories and peoples and their elites, with various parts of the empire sending representatives to the Ottoman parliament. The Ottoman elite was an evolving one based on a culture of empire, rather than on a narrow and exclusive notion of ethnicity or race.

Towards the end of its existence, at a time of increasing weakness and crisis, the nature of the Ottoman Empire did begin to change. As far as the Arabs were concerned, this occurred in two ways. First, the empire attempted to become more centralized and interventionist. This strategy was implemented through the *Tanzimat* or 'reorganization'. In addition to an increasing centralization in administration, the state tried to increase its penetration of the outlying areas of the empire, through the improvement of communications and the extension of a military presence. Ultimately, there was greater willingness to use a modernized army to impose more firmly the authority of the centre. Though the reforms were forged in the early nineteenth century, the mid to latter part of the century is better known as the 'age of the Tanzimat'.[2] For instance, the construction of the Hijaz railway, one of the better-known consequences of the *Tanzimat* philosophy, was completed in 1908. Thus the effects of the new strategy were being felt on the ground during a period when Arab nationalist ideas were beginning to take root among the educated, urban Arab intelligentsia. Just as Arabs were starting to discover themselves as a nation, the Ottoman Empire was becoming increasingly less accommodating.

The second major change in the empire was the emergence of the Young Ottoman movement. Despite the initial pan-Ottoman and liberal inclinations of its Committee for Union and Progress (CUP), it soon became apparent that this movement was more preoccupied with the Turkic peoples of the empire. According to one writer, who shows sympathy for an Arab perspective, 'the CUP was really concerned with promoting a racial policy of pan-Turkism or unity of all Turkish-speaking peoples in Asia'.[3] As the remaining European provinces of the empire were lost while the Young Ottomans were in power, the frictions within the empire increasingly assumed an Arab–Turk dimension. State policies became increasingly illiberal and repressive, with self-consciously politically active Arabs bearing much of the brunt.[4] As a result, many of the emerging Arab political groupings were forced to operate underground. The final two decades of the Ottoman Empire were increasingly unpleasant for the Arab nationalist movement.

Arab–Turkish relations became more and more uneasy in the early twentieth century. Arab resentment at the stultifying political atmosphere of the empire grew alongside increasing introspection on the part of the newly self-conscious Turkish elites. This growing self-preoccupation and its by-product of dwindling interest in the aims and aspirations of the Arab members of the empire was on the whole free of any profoundly negative attitudes towards the Arabs as a community. This changed with the onset of World War I.

When the Great War broke out the Ottoman Empire attempted to portray the conflict as a struggle between the pan-Islamism of the empire and the Christian forces of the Triple Entente. The vast majority of Ottoman subjects, regardless of their ethnic background, tended to accept this characterization at face value. A notable exception was the Sherif of Mecca, who used the conflict to advance his dynastic aspirations to lead an independent Arab state. After secret correspondence with the British, he declared the 'Great Arab Revolt' in 1916. This was a major strategic reverse for the Ottomans, establishing an extra front far distant from the main areas of conflict. It stretched the Ottoman military by opening up the fighting in hostile terrain where supply lines and communications were difficult to maintain. The Sherifian revolt's main material contributions were the seizure of Aqaba and the support of Allenby's push up to Damascus. Furthermore, the intervention of the Sherif's Arab irregulars subverted the Ottoman claim that the war represented a struggle between *dar al-Islam* (the house of Islam) and *dar al-harb* (the house of war).

Though the Ottoman Empire disintegrated soon after the end of the war and a new Turkish republic, with different leaders and a very different ideology, appeared soon after, the Turkish people still tend to regard the Arab uprising as a monumental act of betrayal. In the aftermath of the creation of the modern Turkish state its leaders, as the former president, Celal Bayar, has pointedly confirmed, 'were not disposed ... to re-establish a close relationship with a nation [the Arabs] which had "stabbed the Turkish nation in the back"'.[5] Some 70 years later, it is still normal for educated Turks to refer to the experiences of World War I as definitive proof of the essential untrustworthiness of the Arabs.[6]

The Arab perception of the Ottoman Empire has become more hostile over time. The Arabs have been ever less willing to regard the period as that of two peoples living together on the basis of equality as fellow Muslims. After Arab independence, their view of the empire became progressively more jaundiced, especially as they had to grapple with issues of economic strategy. There was a tendency to blame the underdevelopment of the new Arab states on Ottoman policies that starved Arab provinces of funds, which went instead to other parts of the empire. Some Turkish scholars have attempted to clarify these perceptions, claiming that in the early to mid years of the empire the Arab provinces did experience prosperity and growth.[7] The recent reopening of the debate in Turkey on the impact of the empire on the Arab territories is a response to this increasingly negative view. Such writings tend to confirm the Arab perception that economic exploitation did occur in the latter stages of the empire.

The Ottoman legacy for Turco-Iranian relations has been more subtle. Tension and competition characterized the relationship during the empire, and there were intermittent conflicts. Despite many attempts, however, the Ottomans were never successful in subjugating Persia. Indeed, the existence of a strong Persia on the empire's eastern flank dissipated military resources at a time when the Ottomans were expanding into Europe. Eventually, it 'contributed indirectly to the eventual repulsion' of the Ottoman advance in Europe.[8] Contemporary Turco-Iranian relations are set against this long history of struggle for regional pre-eminence. The residue of two former empires still exerts considerable regional influence and pervades contemporary relations. Both Persian and Turk feel a sense of superiority in the area, which inevitably places them in a competitive mode.

The legacy of the Ottoman–Persian interaction is not universally negative. First, the balanced nature of the historical relationship provides the basis for a balanced contemporary relationship as long as each side takes into account the other's self-interest. The fact that Persia and an Ottoman state have formed two discrete areas since the early Safavids, prior to the sixteenth century, is proof of the autonomy of the two entities. It is therefore more likely that bilateral relations can be developed on the basis of mutual respect by two independent, strong states. There is no legacy of resentment, as with the Arabs, to be exorcised in contemporary relations. As a result, Turkey and Iran have twice since the breakup of the Ottoman Empire been able to enter into alliances based on a strategic convergence, first in 1937 (the Saadabad Pact) and second in 1955 (the Baghdad Pact). Although the Islamic revolution in Iran in 1979 complicated the relationship, creating a new level of antagonism and mistrust and rendering bilateral cooperation less easy, the general legacy of competition among equals still remains.

Second, from a more practical political point of view, the broad historical balance of power between the Ottoman and Persian entities has ensured that boundary problems, so pervasive in the region, have been minimal. In fact the Turkish–Iranian border is one of the oldest borders between two countries in the world.[9] Significantly, it was the only boundary of the Ottoman Empire not to change with the emergence of the modern Turkish state.[10] Given that Turkey has latent border problems with both Syria and Iraq, the solidity of the Turkish–Iranian border gives some succour to a country well-used to difficult relations with its neighbours on all sides.

Disputed territories

During the first two decades of the modern Turkish state two major territorial disputes came to the fore. The first surrounded the frontier between Turkey and Iraq over the status of Mosul. The second and later dispute was between Turkey and Syria and focused on the Sanjak of Alexandretta, or Hatay as it subsequently became known in Turkish. Both issues caused bitter controversy at the time. And both, though not necessarily of central political importance today, contain considerable latent tension, and continue to engender suspicion and resentment towards Turkey on the part of the two Arab states concerned.

Mosul

It has already been noted that the Turkish state emerging out of the Ottoman Empire at one stage promised to be small and vulnerable. The inability of the victorious powers to impose the 1920 Treaty of Sèvres settlement on the Turks owed much to the military power and resolve of the leaders of the republican movement. It was not until the Treaty of Lausanne in July 1923 that the borders of Turkey were recognized by the international community, and established by international law. There was one exception. The negotiations failed to resolve the future of Mosul between Turkey, which claimed the area, and Great Britain, which held the League of Nations mandate for Iraq, and which sought its incorporation in the mandatory area. The future of Mosul was referred for bilateral discussion with a nine-month guillotine.

The Turkish argument for the incorporation of Mosul was that the majority of its population was Kurdish, like that of the adjacent area in Turkey. The Ankara government felt that the integration of the Anatolian

Kurds would be hampered by the presence of an estimated half million unintegrated Kurds next door.[11] In addition, there was a sizeable Turcoman population in Mosul. Actually, the vehemence of the argument on both sides reflected the pre-eminence of the Mosul oilfields in the minds of both sets of negotiators. With talks deadlocked, the issue went to the Council of the League of Nations, which, unsurprisingly given the status of the respective states, found in Britain's favour. The Turks eventually accepted the status of Mosul, albeit reluctantly, and signed a treaty to that effect with Britain and Iraq in June 1926.

Turkey claims that it does not now have any practical designs on Mosul, though its loss may still be a matter for deep regret. Undoubtedly Turkey has lost out economically to a dramatic extent by not having possession of Mosul. Furthermore, Turkish anxiety about the division of the Kurdish area has been shown to be justified. Concern by Turkey over the wellbeing of the Turkic minority in Iraq was also justified given the treatment periodically meted out to them during the Ba'thist era.

The economic, security and demographic implications of the loss of Mosul for Turkey continue to excite Iraqi suspicions about Ankara's ultimate ambitions over the area. An increase in pan-Turkic sentiment and political organization in Turkey, or indeed in the Turkic republics of the Soviet Union, would probably further alarm any regime in Baghdad. Underlying all these problems is the vexed question of how far modern Iraq has become consolidated as a nation-state. In the five-year period between 1985 and 1990 the cohesion of the Iraqi state has twice come into question: first during the height of the fighting in the Iran–Iraq war in 1985 and 1986, when there was a real prospect of the collapse of the Iraqi state in the face of a strong external onslaught; and second in the aftermath of the Iraqi invasion of Kuwait, when a powerful international force assembled in the Arabian Peninsula and the Persian Gulf. The devastating repeated military strikes against Iraq have raised again the possibility of the disintegration of central authority in Baghdad.

Should the Iraqi state fall apart, it is by no means clear what the Turkish reaction would be. Between 1986 and early 1988 there existed considerable uncertainty in the West on this question. This uncertainty was increased by some bellicose opinions in the Turkish press and some ambivalent statements by certain Turkish politicians. For instance, in November 1986, Turkish Prime Minister Turgut Özal, while categorically denying that his country had any plans regarding Kirkuk, nevertheless indicated that Ankara could adopt a more active policy if its security were threatened.[12] There was similar ambivalence after August

1990, prompting speculation that a breakdown in central authority in Iraq might lead to a Turkish occupation of the north, with international complicity, to secure the oilfields and supply routes. Uncertainty surrounded the extent of Turkish intervention if the Kurds of northern Iraq attempted to establish an independent state.

Alexandretta/Hatay

Turkey was more fortunate over the question of the Sanjak of Alexandretta which, nearly two decades after the formation of the republic, was incorporated into the modern state.[13] The material outcome may have fulfilled Turkish objectives, but it was regarded negatively by Syria, to which the Sanjak was formerly attached, and by the Arabs in general.

As with the British over Mosul, Turkey did not originally pursue the question of the Sanjak to the point of arousing international hostility. In 1921 Ankara agreed a compromise with the French, who had received the mandate for the whole of Syria from the League of Nations. Turkey recognized that the Sanjak should be administered under the terms of the mandate in return for extensive cultural concessions to the large Turkish population in the Sanjak. (Controversy still surrounds the question of whether the Turks or the Arabs were the largest single group in Alexandretta/Hatay at the time of its incorporation into Turkey.[14]) By virtue of a leasing accord, the agreement also recognized the importance to Turkey of the port of Alexandretta, its workable outlet on the Mediterranean.[15] The political status of the Sanjak was slightly confused by the agreement that it should have its own flag (incorporating, moreover, the Turkish flag),[16] although the area was subsequently administered as an integral part of Syria. In return for these concessions the Turkish government declared at Lausanne that it renounced 'all rights and title' to the territories south of the frontier, which included the Sanjak.[17]

The arrangement worked well enough until 1936 when the French proposed to grant independence to a Syria that would include the Sanjak. This greatly perplexed Ankara. In contrast to the situation in 1921, Turkey's integration into the world community of states was long completed. There were thus fewer external constraints on Turkish policy than when the question of the Sanjak first arose. Moreover, France had shown its conciliatory and pacific approach to foreign relations by refraining from the use of force over the German reoccupation of the Rhineland. Fortunately for Turkey the backdrop to the future of the Sanjak was a deteriorating political situation in Europe. Britain and France began to court Turkey, which was not aligned to any major European power.

Distracted by the European theatre and eager to placate Turkey, the French effectively created the circumstances under which the Turkish army could march into the Sanjak and in 1939 formally incorporate it as Hatay into the republic.

Syria, which was still not independent from France, regarded this annexation as a gross abuse of the mandate. It was also 'greatly resented by the Arabs' in general.[18] It exposed the lofty claims of the world powers and their essentially colonial and self-interested approach to the Middle East. Turkey, as the beneficiary of this French perfidy, was tarred with the same brush. Ankara had initially operated a double standard over foreign administration of the Turkish population in the Sanjak: it was prepared for the French to rule the Turks there under the terms of the mandate, but balked at their being governed by Arabs. Furthermore, the Turks had shown the Syrians that matters of national interest, such as the need to maintain control over the port, took precedence over general principles on the limitation of Turkish borders. Indeed, wherever there existed a significant Turkish population the rationale existed for the expansion of the state.

The Syrians refused to accept the loss of the Sanjak. The area of Hatay continues to be shown as Syrian on postage stamps and maps produced in Syria. The issue continues to fester under the surface, and to help blight bilateral relations. Even Turkish writers who seek to play down the problems arising over the affair admit that it is still a bone of contention in bilateral relations.[19] There is a strong irredentist feeling among Arab and Syrian nationalists alike in Syria. Periodically, Damascus has stepped up its agitation in Hatay.[20] Furthermore, for a country which aspires to be a regional power the loss of the Sanjak is continuing evidence of the limitation of Syrian strength, and the pre-eminence of Turkish power. For Arab nationalists in general, and their millennial attachment to Arab soil, Turkey's control of the Sanjak is an injustice which should be put right. Despite all the anger and high feeling, however, it is exceptionally unlikely that there will be any physical attempt to wrest back the area, at least in the foreseeable future. With Syria bogged down in Lebanon, and the loss of Palestine being a much greater humiliation for collective Arab pride, Hatay merely continues to be a source of Arab, and particularly Syrian, resentment against Turkey and the Turks.

The Baghdad Pact
It was during the 1950s that Turkey pursued its most active foreign

policy with respect to the Middle East. In 1940 and again in 1945 Turkey had been subjected to concerted demands from the USSR to yield its control of the Straits. Ankara was, therefore, a willing participant in the Cold War on the side of the West. From a Turkish perspective there were two objectives. First, to guard against a direct Soviet attack; it joined Nato, and perceived a strong rationale for banding together with the other regional states of the northern tier to ensure that Moscow would not be able to pick them off individually. Second, there was a need to guard against indirect threats from Soviet proxy states. For most of Western Europe the communist threat was one that emanated essentially from the east. For Turkey this was not the case. It had a number of newly independent states to its south and was concerned to ensure their freedom from Soviet influence so as to reduce any possible threat to itself from that direction. To the Turkish authorities, the Middle East was 'a gap in the line of defence which must be filled'.[21]

As the only Nato member in the Middle East, Turkey seemed to approach the affairs of the region with a sense of moral and political superiority. It appeared to see itself as the Nato vehicle in the region, and certainly made the running, often well ahead of Britain for instance, in trying to galvanize the Middle East into an anti-Soviet alliance. The problem with such a one-track approach was that it did not take into account the interests, priorities and perceptions of the Arab states. Turkey consistently failed to appreciate that for the Arabs Britain and France were colonial powers, from which other Arab territories were, in the 1950s, still attempting to gain their independence. Ankara also failed to understand that the US was seen as the chief guarantor of the state of Israel and was becoming increasingly unpopular as it replaced Britain as the most influential Western power in the region.

Turkey's active diplomacy resulted in the conclusion of a pact of mutual cooperation with Iraq, signed in February 1955. Iraq, under a Hashemite monarchy owing its position to the British, and governed by the Western-oriented Nuri al-Sa'id, was a willing partner for Ankara. This alliance became the nucleus of the Baghdad Pact, which was enlarged to include Britain, Iran and Pakistan later the same year. Jordan would also have joined in 1955 but for internal weakness, and there were hopes of wooing Syria. The Turks were proud of their achievement in establishing a northern tier, and of linking Nato and the South-East Asia Treaty Organization (SEATO) through the membership of Pakistan and Turkey in the same alliance.[22] The Turkish government failed to appreciate the sense of discomfort or even threat which other, more radical and

25

less Western-oriented Arab regimes would feel as the pact was expanded. In particular, they also failed to grasp the political mood sweeping through the Arab world, regardless of the complexion of the regimes in power. Thus, for example, in trying to stampede Jordan into the alliance Turkey almost precipitated the downfall of the monarchy.

Up to this point, Turkey had resolutely insisted that the Baghdad Pact was not aimed at the Arab League or any of the political groups in the region. Its only objective was 'to deter a potential aggressor'.[23] However, after 1956 Turkey became markedly more interventionist in its Middle East policy. There was probably no single cause, but it owed much to increasing alarm in Ankara at a range of developments in the region. Czechoslovakia's arms sales to Egypt, followed by the promise of Soviet finance to help build the Aswan High Dam, no doubt alerted Turkey to the communist penetration of the Arab world. A rapidly emerging arms and economic relationship between Syria and the Soviet Union brought Moscow's involvement to the southern Turkish border. The reverses for Britain and France at the hands of Egypt, both in terms of the nationalization of the Suez Canal and the subsequent débâcle, added to the sense that the West's grasp on the Middle East was slipping. Chronic instability in Jordan and in 1958 in Lebanon heightened the sense of crisis, which culminated in the overthrow of the Iraqi regime in the middle of that year.

Between 1957 and 1959 Turkey increasingly favoured a policy of confronting what was perceived as the communist threat. Perhaps the gravest situation developed in Syria in summer and autumn 1957. Turkey attempted to galvanize both the USA and the Arab states to redress what it saw as the threatened encirclement of the eastern flank of Nato. In the wake of Arab reluctance to put pressure on Syria, Turkey 'seems to have considered the possibility of "going it alone" against Syria'.[24] The crudeness of the Turkish response simply played into Soviet hands. Syria became more dependent on Moscow as the threat from Turkey intensified. For instance, the USSR took the major step of sending a small naval unit to Syria, 'a show of force hitherto unprecedented in a Middle Eastern ... crisis'.[25] Moscow also warned that any aggression against Syria 'would not remain limited to this area alone'.[26] The whole episode permitted the USSR to make 'adroit propaganda', presenting itself as 'the friend of a nationalist Syrian regime threatened by "warmongering imperialists and their tools"'.[27] It also served to strengthen the Soviet Union's position in Syria, with which in October 1957 it concluded a $579 million economic and technical agreement.

Turkey also appeared willing to intervene militarily in Iraq, both in the aftermath of the anti-monarchist revolution and subsequently. The destruction of the Iraqi royal family and the West's faithful servant, Nuri al-Sa'id, in the republican takeover in July 1958 was profoundly disturbing to the Turkish government. It extinguished Turkey's only close ally in the Arab world, as well as removing Baghdad from the Baghdad Pact. Worse still, it threatened to add another communist or communist-controlled country to Turkey's long border with the Iron Curtain states. The meeting of the three remaining local Baghdad Pact powers, which took place directly after the *coup d'état*, resulted in 'some highly unrealistic suggestions' to the USA and the UK 'for military action'.[28] The response was discouraging. The three powers were, however, somewhat reassured by the subsequent airlifting of US and British troops to Lebanon and Jordan respectively to shore up the existing regimes there. Turkey's desire to give practical assistance was fulfilled by the use of the Adana air base to facilitate the transit of American troops. Despite the experiences with Syria and Iraq in the aftermath of the revolution, Ankara still did not appear totally deterred from pursuing a military adventure. In the first few weeks of 1959 it was alarmed at the growing influence of the communists in Iraq and the apparent increased dependence upon them of the new Iraqi leader, Abdul Karim Qasim. Once again, both the USA and the UK were obliged to state unequivocally that 'any idea of intervention [in Iraq] by Iran or Turkey would be most unfortunate'.[29]

Turkey's blinkered and proactive policy towards the Middle East passed with the downfall of the government of Prime Minister Adnan Menderes in 1960. Indeed, towards the end of the 1950s the bipartisan approach in Turkey towards foreign policy had already shown signs of cracking because of opposition reservations at the government's handling of the Middle East.[30] For the next three decades Turkish policy towards the region was markedly more cautious, even to the point of meek-ness. Ankara has been particularly concerned to distance itself where necessary from the policies of its Nato allies. Nevertheless, the Turkish policies of the 1950s are still close enough to remain fresh in the collec-tive Arab mind. Indeed, these were the politically formative years of most Arab heads of state today. Inevitably, the more proactive, less sensi-tive actions and diplomacy of the Turkish government are remembered most vividly. Overlaid upon a deep Arab resentment of the Turks stemming from the latter stages of the Ottoman period, and focused in particular on the outstanding questions of Mosul and Hatay, the latent mutual antipathy between Turk and Arab is both explicable and enduring.

4

MIDDLE EASTERN ISSUES AND DOMESTIC STABILITY

Within Turkey there exist problems and issues which are popularly identified as Middle Eastern in origin, indicating most graphically that Turkey cannot keep that region at arm's length. The two most important 'Middle Eastern issues', which are an inseparable part of Turkey's internal politics, are the Kurdish question and the spread of radical Islam. This chapter considers in particular the threat these pose to the Turkish state.

The Kurds

Kurdish society

The Kurds of southeast Turkey are the most traditionally structured social group in the whole country. Theirs is a predominantly rural society, where kinship ties continue to be the main social cement. The socio-economic structure of the area is divided between a large small-holding peasantry, and a small class of big landowners which employs hired labour. According to 1985 figures, 2 per cent of landowners owned some 30.5 per cent of cultivable land.[1] In general these large landowners are also traditional tribal chiefs, or *aghas*, who have registered large tracts of tribal land in their own names. In recent years these powerful landowners have increasingly consolidated and diversified their wealth by developing broader business interests. The state, whether Ottoman or Turkish, has worked through the *aghas*. This has helped maintain their political importance at a time when the state has taken over from the tribe as the dominant form of political organization. Thus, in the Kurdish areas, there tends to be a potent convergence of social standing and economic and political power, which both bolsters the position of the *aghas* and maintains the loyalty of the communities over which they have historically held sway.

The enduring nature of the old social patterns is not very surprising given the marginal extent of economic change in the area. The Kurdish areas of southeast Turkey remain the most backward in terms of economic development in the republic. Turkey's rapid rise in prosperity during the 1980s has not narrowed the gap between the rural Kurdish areas and the rest of the country. Per capita income in eastern Turkey is only about 40 per cent of the national average.[2] Disparities between the richer and poorer provinces are even starker. For instance, in 1986 GDP per capita in the southeastern province of Hakkari was less than 6 per cent of that in the province of Kocaeli on the Bosporus.[3] This economic underdevelopment is compounded by the poor infrastructure of the southeast. In a country which in recent times has made great strides in terms of industrial output, it is all the more surprising that industry is almost totally absent, even from such a regional centre as Diyarbakır.[4] Apart from the *aghas*, the only Kurds to have prospered during the past decade are those who have left the land for the cities (and it is noteworthy that Istanbul is now the Turkish city with the largest Kurdish population).

The rural Kurdish areas are just as backward in their social development. Educational standards, for instance, are far lower in eastern and southeastern Anatolia than in the rest of Turkey.[5] This is to a large extent a result of the scant resources available and lower investment made there. Many of the remote Kurdish villages do not have schools. Trained teachers are unwilling to work in these mountainous, sparsely populated areas, where, moreover, the return on educational investment is likely to be lower than in more densely peopled regions.[6] Nevertheless, the ambivalence of many Kurds towards the Turkish state, and the Turks' social snobbery towards such backward and underdeveloped regions and their people, make it harder for these areas to use the political process to gain more resources for social projects. The state in turn has been guilty not so much of malevolence as of neglect, and of a general unwillingness to offer positive incentives directly to develop the region. The factors which have caused and which perpetuate the underdevelopment of the east and southeast are many and complex, but the entrenched interests of the local *aghas* and the *shaikhs* of the religious establishment are a recurring theme. The fact that the leading political parties have consistently gone about trying to win votes in these areas simply by working through the traditional socio-economic and religious hierarchies has helped perpetuate structural underdevelopment. The parties coopt the *aghas* and *shaikhs* to deliver votes; in return state resources in cash and material are distributed through these traditional networks. It therefore remains extremely difficult for a political party to set about political reform in the southeast because the organized interests in the area will immediately rebound in the ballot box. Any efforts at reform are implemented feebly, rendering them little more than gestures. The failure of land reform, most recently attempted in 1978, illustrates the underlying failure of political will on the part of the centre to undermine the power of the landlords.

Even though the alliance between the state and the traditional foci of authority in the Kurdish areas cuts across the ethnic divide, the predominantly Kurdish areas of Turkey are readily identified as those which are economically and developmentally dispossessed. Significantly, 'the economic frontier between the least-developed provinces and the remainder of Turkey roughly corresponded to the ethnic divide between the Turkish majority and the Kurdish-speaking minority of eastern and southeastern Anatolia.'[7] This coincidence of economic and human geography has presumably not been lost on the Kurdish nationalist movement.

The insurgency

There has always been a sense of ambivalence on the part of the Kurdish population towards the modern Turkish state. In the early years of the republic this took the form of a dervish-based uprising to protest against the abolition of the Caliphate and the crackdown on all manifestations of a Kurdish identity.[8] In the 1950s and early 1960s, as we shall see below, the Turkish state forged a more extensive accommodation with the traditional leadership in the rural Kurdish areas, by giving them more systematic access to formal political power through, for instance, membership of Turkish political parties.

The cooption of the traditional Kurdish elites by the state helped to turn Kurdish dissidents towards quasi-leftist ideas. In the late 1960s, this synthesis of Kurdish national awareness and radical left-wing ideology resulted in an increase in political activism and some mass demonstrations. The army intervention of March 1971 suppressed the political-cum-cultural groups which had begun to flourish. The declaration of martial law in the Kurdish provinces in 1979 and the military intervention of September 1980 amounted to an assertion that the state 'intended to brook no expression of the Kurdish movement or identity whatsoever'.[9]

The current insurgency is led by the Kurdistan Workers' Party (PKK), an organization which has grown out of this dual tradition of Kurdish nationalism and neo-Marxism. The PKK was formally established in 1979 under the leadership of Abdullah Ocalan.[10] Its ultimate goal is the establishment of a greater independent Kurdistan comprising the Kurdish areas of Turkey, Iraq, Iran and Syria. Its avowed medium-term goal appears more realistic. According to the leader of the PKK: 'There's no question of separating from Turkey. My people need Turkey: we can't split for at least 40 years.'[11] The main tactics of the PKK have been to proclaim armed struggle against Turkish 'colonialism' and the Kurdish 'feudalism' which supports it. It has at various times enjoyed sanctuary in parts of Syria and the no man's land of northern Iraq and Iran, in addition to Lebanon, where its main training bases are to be found. The operative strength of the PKK is difficult to estimate. In the past it has been conventionally numbered at between 2,000 and 3,000 men but recent reports suggest it could have grown to as many as 5,000.[12]

The PKK began its insurgency campaign in August 1984. Its operations have consisted of small groups of PKK activists primarily engaged in hit-and-run raids directed mainly against soft targets, both human and material. The majority of their victims have been Kurdish employees of the state, in either the military or the civilian sector, such as schoolteachers, engineers or their families.[13] The aim has been to terrorize the population into severing its links with the Turkish state. The high Kurdish casualty rate reflects the fact that 70 per cent of the civil service in the southeast of the country is ethnically Kurdish, and that there exists an 18,000-strong armed civilian guard.[14] Total casualty figures vary wildly. By late spring 1990 estimates for those killed during the insurgency ranged between 1,245 and 5,000.[15] The activities of the PKK have been concentrated spatially on the border areas of southeast Turkey, and seasonally in the spring and summer. The mountainous terrain makes it extremely difficult for the security forces to stop all incursions into the country.

The beginning of the 1990s has witnessed two developments which may prove to be a watershed. First, in 1990 there was a quantitative increase in the intensity of the conflict in the southeast of the country as measured by loss of human life, with 55 deaths in March alone, compared with 16 in the first quarter of the previous year.[16] The mounting casualty figures are not just a result of increased activity by the PKK. They also indicate a more concerted effort by the Turkish security forces to stamp out the incursions, and a higher profile for the Turkish military

31

at the expense of the gendarmerie in the policing operation.

Second, there has been a qualitative change in the nature of the conflict, with the first popular show of support for the insurgents against the Turkish authorities.[17] Mass demonstrations took place in the frontier town of Nusaybin on 15 March 1990, and were followed by a strike by local shopkeepers. Five days later unrest spread to Cizre, a town of similar size, some 90 kilometres to the east. Four people were killed and nine wounded in clashes with the security forces. Government offices were set ablaze, and there was another commercial strike. There were brief demonstrations in Istanbul. Shops were shut down for a short period in the Kurdish regional city of Diyarbakır.

This outburst of civil protest has been described by Kurds in Turkey as an *intifada*, an allusion to the uprising in the occupied territories in which Palestinians armed with stones have confronted the Israeli army. The violence in Cizre, during which 20 were claimed killed by Kurdish sources, has been dubbed the 'Kurdish Timisoara'[18] – a reference to the city where the popular demonstrations against the Romanian president, Nicolae Ceaucescu, began the previous December. The sporadic nature of the popular demonstrations indicates that comparisons with the Palestinian *intifada* are exaggerated. To assess whether they are merely premature, one must consider the response of the Turkish state to the activities of the PKK and its likely long-term effects.

The response of the Turkish state

The Turkish state has attempted to deal with its Kurdish problem in three ways. First, it has sought to integrate its Kurdish population into the economic and political life of the country on its own Turkish terms. Second, it has addressed the specific problem of Kurdish political violence. Third, it has sought to tackle the economic underdevelopment in the Kurdish east and southeast.

The integration of the Kurds is a policy which has been pursued explicitly in the political domain and implicitly in the economic sphere. As already indicated, in the 1950s and 1960s there was a conscious effort by the state to coopt Kurdish notables into the political process. Kurds responded favourably to the first free general election in 1950, and the victorious Democratic Party was well supported in the rural Kurdish areas. This marked the beginning of an effective partnership between the Kemalist state and the traditional leadership, though always with the former as the dominant partner. Nevertheless, many of these notables were elected to parliament or even became ministers.

The regional imbalances of the Turkish economy prompted considerable internal labour migration. The concentration of industrial and other investment in the west of the country and the relative neglect of the east determined the direction of this migration. The endemic poverty of the rural Kurdish areas meant that the Kurds were often the first to move off the land and seek work in the urban and coastal areas of Turkish Anatolia. The trend was so strong that the majority of the Kurds in Turkey no longer live in the southeast of the country.[19] As one foreign diplomat put it: 'The migration of Kurds from rural to urban areas due to local poverty is comparable to the massive migration of blacks from the south to the industrial north in the US after the Second World War.'[20]

In addressing the problem of Kurdish political violence, the Turkish state has not flinched from confronting violence with violence, and terror with terror. It has also introduced an uncompromising policy aimed at the secondary activity of suspected PKK collaborators and sympathizers. Activity by the intelligence services has increased. Since 1989 the Turkish military has become increasingly involved in trying to reimpose security in the southeast, with an estimated 65,000 Turkish troops posted there before the Gulf crisis began in August 1990. Measures against the civilian population have been highly contentious and arguably even counterproductive. Mass arrests of suspected PKK collaborators and demonstrators have taken place. Detainees have often been kept in custody for days before being released. Torture and beatings are commonplace. Collective punishment is also on the increase, with action against villages suspected of helping the insurgents. Indeed, under cover of the Gulf crisis, a more hardline policy was introduced, with the systematic razing of rural settlements; in August and September 1990 an estimated 27 villages and 80 hamlets in Şımak district were destroyed.

The efficacy of the widespread use of such crude methods of intimidation is highly debatable. The measures appear to have helped politicize and then radicalize different constituencies of the Kurdish people, particularly the young, who have been at the forefront of the demonstrations. This radicalization has also extended spatially from the border areas to some of the principal Kurdish towns. If the Kurdish community has indeed been radicalized and polarized by the repression, the Turkish state apparatus will have aided the cause of the PKK, which has presumably used violence both in order to polarize the Kurdish community and to produce an indiscriminate backlash on the part of the Turkish military authorities.

In the wake of the popular demonstrations, the Turkish state published a controversial draconian decree, Kararname 413,[21] which has supplemented the military approach to the conflict with a range of ancillary measures. This decree in part aimed to retain the loyalty of Kurdish state officials in the stricken areas through the provision of higher salaries. However, the real thrust of the package was twofold: first, to increase the punitive effect of measures that could be applied in the problem areas; and second, to control the flow of information on events there through greatly increased restrictions on the media. The enhanced powers of the regional governor included stiffer penalties for insurgents and those who aid and abet them, the ability to exile people outside the area, and the authority to ban strikes and lockouts.

Media restrictions have been sweeping. The state broadcasting authority, TRT, is now effectively subject to the veto of the Ministry of the Interior and the National Security Council. The restrictions on the press, which is traditionally inquiring and independent in Turkey, are likely to have more far-reaching implications. The Interior Ministry has the powers to ban and confiscate publications and close down printing presses, regardless of their location, in the event of their giving false information on events in the troubled southeast, spreading alarm and despondency or hindering the operations of the security forces. The ministry itself remains the ultimate judge of such issues. Its strict control means it is now very much more difficult to obtain information on the area, let alone to evaluate it correctly.

The Turkish state has turned its attention rather belatedly to the question of economic underdevelopment in the region. The chief policy formulated in part to achieve this objective is the Southeast Anatolian Project (GAP). GAP is a $20 billion integrated venture which will provide for the construction of 21 dams and 17 hydroelectric power plants.[22] The assumption is that the creation of an advanced agricultural and utilities infrastructure will lead to both greater employment opportunities and greater prosperity for the 4.5 million people in the proposed catchment area. The central political premise upon which this policy initiative is based is that while the rural Kurdish areas remain poor the inhabitants will be susceptible to subversive nationalist and neo-Marxist ideology; conversely, a thriving local economy, replete with job opportunities and higher incomes, would strongly discourage the local population from flirting with such radical and destabilizing forces.

Even assuming that this political premise is valid, there are a number of problems with the project. The first is its scope. Despite the massive nature of the undertaking, in terms of both area and capital investment,

GAP will lead to the transformation of the economy in only six provinces.* Though the benefits can be expected to filter down, economic rejuvenation elsewhere in the rural Kurdish areas will be more modest.

The second problem relates to exactly how much investment the state will deliver. Work has moved on apace on the large, prestige engineering projects such as the Atatürk Dam and the Urfa irrigation tunnel. Officials and businessmen in Ankara and Istanbul speak with pride of such large-scale achievements. Yet it cannot be assumed that all the dams will be built. Much will depend upon the health of the Turkish economy when subsequent investments are due to be made. In addition, large engineering structures and huge reservoirs are less likely to impress local people. For them, the extension of electricity, the building of roads, and the provision of irrigation water will be the yardsticks against which the policy is judged. In these areas, the state has been rather less conscientious and effective. By spring 1990 the major opposition politicians in Turkey had come to appreciate this and were making domestic political capital out of it.[23]

The third problem relates to the ownership of the land affected by the GAP project. In the past, much of it belonged to large landowners. The issue of land ownership and redistribution remains ill-defined. Officials appear reluctant to discuss it in detail. Rumours abound of speculators buying land in the designated areas on the assumption that it will be a much more productive resource when the GAP scheme is implemented. Even if the land should remain in the hands of the few, whether traditional or new owners, there would still be a trickle-down effect. However, the increased levels of prosperity which are being promised would not under these circumstances come about, and expectations would have been raised unrealistically.

The fourth problem is with the timing of the project. Turkey's agricultural and agro-industrial potential will not be significantly enhanced by GAP before the mid 1990s, when 'serious agro-industrial investment begins in the GAP region'.[24] It is uncertain how quickly private-sector investment will be attracted to the area. The lead time until this investment begets profit and a general improvement in the wealth of the area can also only be a matter of guesswork. What is clear is that the major economic benefits envisaged will not accrue before 1995 and probably not until after the year 2000. Thus the GAP project offers little hope for

*The six provinces are Adiyaman, Diyarbakır, Gaziantep, Mardin, Şanlıurfa and Siirt. The province of Hakkari, where many of the PKK operations have taken place, is not included.

improving the conditions which have brought about extensive hostility in the Kurdish areas to the Turkish state at the beginning of the 1990s.

Future prospects

There seems little doubt that the insurgency in southeast Turkey will continue, probably for as long as the PKK receives sanctuary in neighbouring countries and passive assistance in Turkey from sections of the Kurdish population. Both of these factors at present appear assured. Indeed, the outburst of popular feeling in spring 1990 suggests that an increasing proportion of younger, urban-based Kurds are implacably alienated from the Turkish state. This constituency could provide a fertile recruiting ground for Kurdish nationalist and other opposition groups. It also suggests that the intensity of violence which marked the early months of 1990 could, in a sporadic and seasonal form, be the new norm. The outpouring of resentment indicated that the Turkish state has lost the battle for the hearts and minds of a large section of the Kurdish population in this part of the country. The blanket, hardline approach of the Turkish armed forces and government has done much to foster this deep-seated disaffection.

Nevertheless, the insurgency and resulting instability do not, at present, pose a real threat to the integrity of the Turkish state. The number of insurgents is too small and the Turkish army too powerful. It is difficult to imagine the PKK being in a position to declare any segment of even southeast Turkey a liberated area. Its statements about not seeking secession in the medium term make a virtue of necessity. It is unlikely that any of Turkey's neighbours would want to see the Turkish state under threat. For Iraq and Iran there are serious domestic implications; Syrian leverage is at its height when the PKK is dependent upon it for a military base.

Instability and discontent in the Kurdish rural areas are, however, likely to damage the Kemalist ideology of the Turkish state. The growing alienation of large numbers of Kurds from the institutions of the Turkish state and the Turkish identity which pervades them highlights the myth of a national consensus based on a Turkish cultural foundation. The polarization of Turkish and Kurdish cultural and even political aspirations could lead to further unease and confrontation. If this comes about, Turkey risks completing the process of creating a Kurdish national movement out of a set of disparate tribes, in much the same way as the Iraqi state appears to have done. If such a movement takes hold, outbreaks of unrest could spread to Kurdish communities elsewhere in Anatolia, especially in the big cities and the universities.

The Turkish state could face more far-reaching reverses than even those being sustained by its ideology. The reputation of the Turkish military, both the creator and the guarantor of the state, is at stake. Respect for the army in Turkey will hinge increasingly on the level of violence in the Kurdish areas as the military steps up its involvement in the suppression of the insurgency. If the army is shown to be largely ineffective against a guerrilla campaign its reputation will be tarnished. Deep divisions could also emerge both within the army and between it and the civilian government over the conduct of its security campaign. The reputation of Turkey abroad could be further damaged if increasing emphasis is placed on a solution based upon coercion and its corollary, the infringement of human rights.

Some commentators hope that the Turkish state will try to take the political sting out of such a movement by conceding a package of cultural and linguistic concessions to its Kurds. At least one major political party, the Social Democratic Populist Party (SHP), has hinted that it might endorse such a move, though many among Turkey's political and intellectual elites appear to have a long way to go before they accept such a compromise. Even then, a cultural package could be too little too late. New economic investments could be made in the southeast to help alleviate the poverty and unemployment there in order to try to make the population feel that it has a stake in the system. Time, here, is of the essence. GAP is an insufficient response. Its benefits are too long-term to address current political problems. Moreover, the supposed benefits to the small farmer and labourer of such a large-scale, macroeconomic project are not immediately discernible.

Politics and Islam

Atatürk and religion
When the modern Turkish republic was established there existed no blueprint for the separation of secular government from temporal authority in the Islamic world. In pursuing his objectives, Atatürk was guided by two elements: the experience of Christian Europe, and, more importantly, his own highly attuned political sense of what was attainable in the new state of Turkey. The former, though of dubious utility as a model, was important to Atatürk because he believed that the division of church and state had allowed rationalism and science to emerge as leading planks of Western civilization – a development which he

contrasted positively with the dominant role which 'corrupted religion' had played during the Ottoman Empire. For Atatürk the lesson was simple: 'A science-oriented mind was open and inventive; a religion-oriented one was narrow and underdeveloped.'[25] His grasp of what was attainable, however, is still of crucial importance, especially in the continued absence of a model for the separation of the secular and the spiritual under Islam. The relationship between the religious and the secular in Turkey is a fluid one which has seeped, rather than gushed, in both directions at different times over the past 70 years.

Atatürk had a twofold objective as far as religion was concerned: one tactical in a narrow political sense, the other strategic, designed to promote revolutionary change in the cognitive map of the Turkish people. First, as a practical politician concerned with the retention of power, Atatürk sought 'to disengage [Islam] from the condition of being a political instrument'.[26] Second, he wanted to reduce Islam to the level of a 'civic religion', because of what he perceived as its tyranny over the values and thought processes of the Turkish people. He believed, as Ş erif Mardin has put it, that 'Islam as a state religion denied ... autonomy to the citizen'.[27] His aim was therefore nothing less than the transformation of what was to him a corporate body of superstitious God-fearers into a community of individual citizens.

If any one leader could have achieved it, Atatürk could. He approached his aim with a politically potent combination of tactical prudence and brazen audacity. He did not attempt to introduce all his reforms simultaneously.[28] When he did decide that the time was opportune, he was courageous and committed in the implementation of reform. Nevertheless, his success in his two objectives was shallow and uneven.

He was successful in ensuring that Islam could not be used in the political process to threaten his position or his cherished reforms during his lifetime. This he accomplished through sheer force of personality, driving Islamic symbols and ideas beyond the parameters of political debate, and suppressing the *tarikat*. However, Islam as a political resource was only lying dormant. The religious orders were forced underground, not destroyed. The eclipse of religion as a political tool was more revealing for what it showed of Atatürk's personal authority and political will than for any change in Islam and the political process during the first generation of the new state.

With regard to his strategic aim, the creation of the autonomous citizen, Atatürk's impact was a curious mixture of total success and total failure. Among the military, the intelligentsia, and in the major cities

Atatürk's impact was profound; it is these communities which worship him still. The contrast is acute with the peasantry in rural areas and increasingly with the new rural migrants to the big cities, especially the *gecekondular* (illegal squatter communities). The fez may no longer be worn (although the headscarf often is) and the Latin script may be in use, but the values and beliefs of such communities have been largely unaffected by Atatürk, his ideas and his reforms.

Rolling back the secular reform

It was only some nine years after the death of Atatürk that his religious reforms began to be rolled back. This suggests that one should regard the first two decades of the republic as the exception rather than a norm which is now suddenly under threat. As soon as President Ismet İnönü decided in 1945 to dispense with one-party rule, Islam re-entered the political domain as an important variable in the competition for power.[29] This was followed two years later by the initial breach in the Atatürk dam of secular reform, as the Ministry of Education accepted new guidelines for the teaching of religion outside schools. Countless piecemeal changes followed, such as the principle that foreign exchange would be available to persons making the pilgrimage to Mecca, and the reopening of the shrines of Muslim saints.

Of considerable symbolic value was the rescinding in 1950 of the requirement that the call to prayer be made in Turkish rather than Arabic. The retraction contained an implicit acknowledgment of the limitations of Mustafa Kemal's Turkism, as well as an acceptance that the state should not seek to regulate every public manifestation of the Islamic religion. The fact that the religious establishment and the public resoundingly reiterated their choice of Arabic as the favoured language for religious observance indicated the likely trend in the absence of a strong lead from the Kemalist state.

Individually, such changes may appear rather insignificant, especially to Western eyes. Taken together, they add up to a tide of re-Islamization which, since the late 1940s, has been edging back up the secular shore. They also indicate the steady impact which a resurgence of Islamism has had upon policy-making in Turkey, and the general inability of the Kemalist establishment, civilian and military, to oppose their implementation.

This flurry of changes was not limited to the period immediately following the emergence of a multi-party democracy in Turkey. It was not a one-off readjustment which diluted the 'extreme Kemalism' and brought Turkey back to a more balanced position between its Islamic

39

tradition and the secular modern reforms.[30] The steady and inexorable nature of the re-Islamization of Turkish society may be seen in the changes in the educational sector over the last four decades. Like other religious zealots the world over, the Islamists in Turkey have targeted education for special priority in the propagation of their ideas. Showing great patience and a strong strategic sense, Islamists have undermined the educational sector in Turkey as a pillar of Kemalism. It has now become fertile ground in which their own ideas can flourish.

The 1947 Ministry of Education guidelines have proved to be small acorns. The oaks are passing into maturity with firm and broadening trunks. Today, Turkey is steadily dismantling the educational system, which even predated Atatürk and is modelled along French and German lines. Religious education pervades the state school system. Indeed, Islamic religious education has even become compulsory for non-Muslims.[31] If resource allocation is the best way to read government priorities, then it is surely significant that in the 1990 budget a 237 per cent increase was made in the funds at the disposal of the Department of Religious Affairs, which runs Turkey's Sunni mosques. This state department is attached to the office of the prime minister, and now has a budget superior to nine full ministries, including those of the interior, and trade and industry.

The state has also permitted the establishment of what David Barchard has described as 'a parallel secondary school system'.[32] So-called vocational schools for imams have been created as an alternative to the existing secondary school sector. These institutions turn out over 50,000 graduates a year,[33] some 13 per cent of all secondary school graduates. The size and productivity of these schools are far in excess of the employment needs or abilities of Turkey's 60,000 mosques,[34] by some ten times according to one commentator.[35] In fact, many of these graduates go on to attend university, where their field of study is unrestricted.

The rolling back of Atatürk's secular reforms has taken place under the stewardship of what is essentially a Kemalist regime. Individual governments, while expressing reverence for Atatürk, have supplied the legislation necessary to effect these changes. The military, though apparently fiercely Kemalist, has watched and even presided over some of this re-Islamization. This paradox needs to be explained, both to understand Turkish politics and to gauge the political will of the Kemalist establishment in opposing future reform.

The original burst of changes towards orthodox Islam in the late 1940s may be explained as a belated reaction to the death of Atatürk.

Mustafa Kemal had dominated Turkish politics during the 1920s and 1930s. The autonomy which he enjoyed within Turkish politics and society was very wide indeed. It was clear at the time of his death that no other figure had his political stature. Certainly no other figure possessed either his personal charm or his political vision, though his successor as president, Ismet İnönü, did share his iron political will. It was only to be expected that Atatürk's death, or certainly the passing of İnönü, would bring safer, more middle-of-the-road policies.

The external political context no doubt helped to precipitate this readjustment. In the late 1940s Turkey was subject to unrivalled Soviet pressure. There was a real prospect of armed conflict as Turkey attempted to resist Moscow's attempts to take control of the Straits. Domestic political divisions would have been an expensive luxury. There was a need not only to build up a political consensus but also to widen the local legitimacy base in order to minimize internal tensions in the face of the external threat. A quick and easy way to court popularity was to relax legislation on the Islamic faith.

These explanations do not, however, show why Islamist inroads into government policy continued over the following 40 years. Three broad explanations may be offered for the continuation of this slow but steady erosion of secularism: first, the desperate search for power followed by the compulsion to retain it on the part of political parties; second, the emergence of the Muslim Middle Eastern oil producers as major power centres in the world economy; and third, the fear of left-wing subversion.

Expedients were readily sought if they facilitated either the pursuit or the maintenance of power. The opportunism reflected in the small tilt towards Islam manifested by the Democratic Party in the late 1940s has since repeatedly been resorted to by Turkish politicians and parties, especially at times of political difficulty. Thus, the Democratic Party had little need to make further concessions to demands for the restoration of Islam during the first years of its decade in power. 'It was later, when things began to go wrong economically, that he [Adnan Menderes] tried to arrest his party's decline by courting the "religious vote".'[36] Such venality was not confined to the early years of Turkish democracy. In the 1970s, when the electoral system in Turkey resulted in a weak multi-partyism, the two major parties successively courted the avowedly Islamist party, the National Salvation Party (NSP), as a coalition partner in order to remain in power. The importance of Islam as a tactical resource of domestic Turkish politics had returned, despite all Atatürk's attempts to banish it.

There was a host of ways in which Turkey, as a comparatively developed state, believed that it could benefit from the capital accumulation of the neighbouring Gulf countries. Predicted benefits included the export of Turkish goods, the attraction of Gulf tourism and capital investment, and the securing of construction contracts which would involve the migration of local Turkish labour.

The promise of these economic rewards necessitated that Turkey project a non-threatening, culturally sympathetic image to the newly wealthy oil states. It was thus important that it play up its Islamic identity at the same time as moderating its secularity. Turkish governments realized that the more overtly Islamic states in the Gulf perceived the Kemalist laicism of Turkey as an alternative model of government. As such, it posed an implicit threat to their own regimes, based as they were upon Islamic legitimacy.[37] This helps to explain Turkey's decision to join the Islamic Conference Organization in 1976. The military must have accepted this rationale, as Turkey's role within the ICO was expanded after the *coup d'état* of 1980. The adoption of policies of a more Islamic bent could, therefore, be justified, by civilian and military politicians alike, on the pragmatic grounds of economic advancement.

There was a further price to pay as a result of this approach. For a regime like the one in Saudi Arabia, which was founded squarely on an Islamic legitimacy, it was deemed important to try to consolidate and deepen the re-Islamization process taking place in Turkey. With its capital windfall, Riyadh had the means to pursue this objective. As a result, Saudi Arabia has pumped large amounts of capital into Turkey since 1975. Much of it has gone towards the overt strengthening of the Islamist movement in the republic. Much of the massive mosque-building programme has been financed by the Saudis. It is also reliably stated that Saudi Arabia gives financial support to the only mainstream Islamist party, the Welfare Party. The moderation of the Kemalist ideology at home in order to secure economic benefit from the Gulf has thus encouraged the Islamizing tendencies of the Saudis.

The third explanation for the re-Islamization policies of the Turkish authorities was the fear of left-wing subversion. When the military intervened in 1980 they were determined to put an end to the violence perpetrated by political groups. It soon became clear, however, that the left was perceived as a greater threat than the right, especially the religious right which had not been involved in the widespread use of political violence in the late 1970s. The military thus regarded the ideas and values of conservative Islam as a bulwark against the perceived growing penetration of society by the plethora of crypto-Marxist groups. So, for instance, while the 1982 constitution imposed severe restrictions on left-wing activity, it also introduced the compulsory teaching of Islam in schools. In addition to a foreign policy more acceptable to the rest of the Islamic world, the early to mid 1980s also saw a loosening of official attitudes towards the *tarikat*, even though they remain formally proscribed.

The threat from political Islam

Since the Iranian revolution, Western strategists have been preoccupied by the 'Islamic threat', especially in traditionally friendly Muslim states. Contemporary analysts are forever being urged to consider whether such states are likely to 'go Muslim'. Since the late 1980s, this is a question which has been asked with greater urgency in relation to Turkey. It has become fashionable once more to speak of Turkey as being increasingly fundamentalist and hence closer to becoming unstable. These concerns are not the exclusive preserve of foreign strategists. The fundamentalist threat exercises the minds of certain groups and strata of the Turkish people. In a rough and ready poll in April 1990, fundamentalism topped the list of issues feared most by a random cross-section of the inhabitants of Istanbul, Ankara and Izmir, outstripping terrorism and even inflation.[38]

What exactly is the nature of the 'Islamic threat' in Turkey? There are three ways in which this may be manifested. First, there could be a direct challenge to the prevailing regime, unmediated by constitutional pro-priety and possibly incorporating the use of political violence. The experience of Iran, where the Shah's regime was confronted openly by mass disaffection, has made the Western press and even policy-makers hawk-eyed to the slightest signs of this. The demonstrations over the 'turban affair' in spring 1989 led to speculation that this was the begin-ning of a mass Islamic movement capable of challenging the very foun-dation of the Kemalist state.[39] One year later commentators were quick to extrapolate about the start of a campaign of violence and terror against their secular opponents by the extremist Islamist fringe. Responsibility for the murder of a handful of intellectuals in 1990, ostensibly for their secular views, was placed at the door of such shadowy groups. However, both cases are based on very limited evidence. The fact that the demon-strations over the turban affair, which in any case never attracted mass participation, evaporated after the resolution of the incident appears to have gone unnoticed. The campaign of assassinations, if indeed it is system-atic enough to be called a campaign, has nowhere threatened to approach the scale of political violence witnessed in Turkey in the late 1970s.

43

The second manifestation could be an electoral challenge posed by Islamists working within the constitution and the due process of law. A major Islamist party has contested most of the free elections in Turkey. In 1973 the leading Islamist party of the day, the National Salvation Party, caused great surprise by taking 11.8 per cent of the vote. That the NSP served in successive left- and right-led coalitions in the mid 1970s underlined its willingness to work within the existing political process.

The main Islamist party in Turkey today is the Welfare Party, the successor to the NSP, led by the veteran Islamist politician, Professor Necmettin Erbakan. In the 1987 election the Welfare Party took 7.2 per cent of the vote. During the local elections of March 1989 its share of the vote rose to 9.5 per cent and it captured more mayorships than the ruling Motherland Party (ANAP). One leading authority described the result as a 'breakthrough' for the party.[40] Although the Welfare Party clearly does not rival the three main political parties in national terms, the figures quoted do not convey its importance. For the Welfare Party's support is not distributed evenly and hence thinly over the country but is concentrated notably in the southeast, where it is now one of the two main parties along with the SHP, and in such areas as the traditionally Islamist province of Konya.

The democratic outlet for Islamists is not confined to the Welfare Party. The Motherland Party itself is a broad-based alliance that includes the Islamic right, a faction which has become increasingly influential. The leading personality on this side of the party is Minister of State Mehmet Keçeciler, the former mayor of Konya. In mid November 1990 the number of cabinet ministers broadly associated with the Islamic right was estimated at between 18 and 20 out of a total of 27.[41] It is practically impossible to estimate what might be the combined Islamist vote in Turkey. The figure might be around 20 per cent, although some local analysts put it as high as 30 per cent. With a turnout in the 1987 general election of just under 24 million, Islamist electoral support could well range between 5 million and 7 million.

Such bald figures should not arouse alarm. With the dominant figure of Turgut Özal installed in the presidency the influence of the cabinet has been marginalized. It is in any case arguably a freakish phenomenon that such a large proportion of the cabinet is identified as Islamist; if the ANAP vote dwindles at the next election, as seems likely, then the Islamists will almost certainly be less well represented in cabinet, almost regardless of the permutation of the next government. Moreover, the Islamist vote is divided between two political parties, and may be expected to remain divided in the future, thereby continuing to weaken its impact.

The third way in which Islamism could manifest itself is through a more subtle, indirect influence upon policy. Reference has already been made to the popularity over the last four decades of a more Islamic-oriented policy within Turkey. Though electors have been wary of voting *en masse* for an Islamist party, they have consistently shown approval when the main political parties have incorporated more Islamic policies into their programmes.

The past decade has also apparently witnessed an increase in personal piety among Turks. There has been a sharp growth in numbers attending mosques and patronizing Islamic schools. There has also been a steady rise in the numbers making the pilgrimage to the Islamic holy places; in 1987 well over 108,000 people travelled from Turkey to attend the *haj* and *'umra* in Saudi Arabia.[42] Furthermore, the re-Islamization of the educational sector, which was begun over 40 years ago, is probably now bearing fruit. The increase in personal piety is unlikely to be ignored by the main political parties. It may well shift the secular–religious balance further towards the religious. The Kemalist policies of the state look likely to be further eroded.

Towards a new balance

Secularism in Turkey is clearly receding before the tide of re-Islamization. The changes have been broadly welcomed and hence legitimized by the Turkish population. The process is steady rather than swift. This is perhaps why the Kemalist establishment and the groups identified with Kemalism have not been more vigorous in their opposition, although the continued erosion of the Kemalist legacy seems certain. The impact of a strongly Islamized educational system will be increasingly profound in the future. The ambivalence towards or rejection of Turkey by the European states, especially the EC, will inevitably focus the Turkish identity more squarely on its non-European attributes. The expected resurgence of the Gulf oil economies, whenever that should occur, as a result of a sustainable increase in oil revenues will rejuvenate the Middle East as an economic power centre, and hence further orient Turkey towards those states.

This almost inevitable expansion of the re-Islamization process in Turkey should not automatically cause dismay among Western strategic thinkers. Islam is an inextricable part of both the Turkish national identity and its culture. To deny this would be self-delusion; to seek to

45

subvert it risks, at best, further distancing much of the population from the philosophy and process of government. Indeed, the trend should be welcomed, with a qualification on the developments in the educational sphere. Progress towards re-Islamization has been sufficiently constant to prevent the emergence of a mass Islamic opposition movement which threatens civil unrest or even the regime itself. The fact that the vast majority of Islamists in Turkey work within the democratic framework of the state should be regarded as a success for the participatory structures. In addition, the movement has been gradual enough to ensure that the Kemalists have been kept on board. During the 1980s at least a working arrangement existed between the religious and secular domains within Turkey, although it is an arrangement slowly evolving in the direction of the former.

The chief question for the future is how much longer the Kemalist establishment and its allies will accept an arrangement which is gradually but inexorably moving against them. As long as the Islamists do not overplay their hand, and simply let the re-Islamization of the population permeate through into policy, the answer appears to be for some time to come. The supplementary question is what the reaction of the Islamists would be if the Kemalist establishment moved away from its conciliatory position. In such a situation of intransigence, and probable confrontation, the stability of Turkey might indeed be in jeopardy.

5

LIVING IN A TOUGH NEIGHBOURHOOD[1]

Most studies of Turkey's foreign policy and relationship with its neighbours tend to focus on Greece and the Soviet Union. While these are important, they do not justify the glaring neglect of Turkey's relations with its southeastern neighbours. Arguably, since the 1974 Cyprus crisis, Turkey's relations with Iraq, Iran and Syria have been subject to greater change and uncertainty than those with Greece or the Soviet Union. In the future, issues such as water, the Kurds, the military balance and the increased prosperity of all three neighbours as oil-producing states will ensure that the Turkey–Iraq–Iran–Syria regional sub-system remains complex and fluid.[2]

There is one further reason for giving more attention to Turkey's relations with its southeastern rather than its western or northern neighbours. Turkey is superior to Greece both in terms of military resources and strategic depth. Though obviously inferior in population and firepower to the Soviet Union, Turkey has enjoyed considerable Western support to bolster its position as regards Moscow. But in its relations with its immediate Middle Eastern neighbours, Turkey is not only in an inferior position but also potentially rather out on a limb. It does not have a strategic advantage – say with regard to population or land size – vis-à-vis Iran, and it is currently militarily inferior to Syria in missile and non-conventional weaponry. But perhaps the greatest differences are psychological. In its dealings with the Middle East states Turkey is out of its political depth. The informal and changeable nature of Middle East politics contrasts with the formalistic legalism of Turkey's political style. Moreover, in its interactions with the Middle East, Turkey has not had an alliance ready to give it support and assistance. Even after the Gulf crisis, Turkey will be unable to rely upon the physical backing of the USA and the European states should other, less clearcut, local difficulties arise in the future.

The regional setting

Turkey's political and intellectual elites do not generally regard themselves as Middle Eastern, while the bulk of the population probably do not much care whether they are or not. Whatever the people's view of themselves, Turkey is part of the Middle East system of states. It may not be a central actor in economic, geographical or ethnic terms, but it is affected by the political currents of the region; and its policies in other areas have implications for its relations with the Middle East. Many Turkish businessmen and some political figures might prefer to have a relationship with the Middle East akin to Japan's: a thriving and complementary economic relationship which avoids, for the most part successfully, questions of a political nature. Though the Japanese model is attractive, it is untenable: Turkey is too close to have the luxury of a Japanese detachment.

Turkey's immediate sphere of concern in the Middle East must be with the states adjacent to it: Syria, Iran and Iraq. From Turkey's point of view, all three share certain characteristics which are potentially problematic. First, all three states have regional leadership aspirations. This means that each state is actively working towards establishing itself as the dominating influence in the area. It also means that because Turkey itself is a regional power there is a tendency on the part of the other three to regard it as a fourth competitor for regional influence.

More tangibly, all three states have the resources to give substance to these ambitions. Historically, both Damascus and Baghdad have been the seats of empires, while both remain regional power centres; the Persian Empire also once dominated the area. The material resources also exist, albeit to varying degrees. With Syrian output increasing, all three are now major oil producers, and also have considerable agricultural potential. All three have substantial populations by regional standards. The populations of Syria and Iraq are of course smaller than those of Iran and Turkey. However, as the Iran–Iraq war showed, a paper population advantage does not automatically equal military supremacy, especially with the regional emergence of non-conventional weapons of mass destruction.

All three have common borders with Turkey. This means that boundary disputes and irredentist movements are more likely to exist; such is the case with Syria and to a lesser degree Iraq. It also means that there are likely to be ethnic and kinship ties which straddle these borders. The existence of Kurdish populations within all four states is the best example of this. It certainly means that it is easier for the neighbouring powers to make mischief within the Turkish border. There also exists the possibility of one neighbouring state attempting to interfere in a second neighbouring state via Turkish territory. The porous nature of the three respective boundaries with Turkey and the mountainous terrain on the Turkish side makes such interference much harder either to monitor or to stamp out.

All three states are formally and instinctively anti-Western. All three have in their recent histories been subject to Western control: Syria and Iraq in the wake of World War I under the cover of the League of Nations mandate system, and Iran less formally both at the hands of the British and, from the early 1950s until the revolution, of the United States. These experiences continue to be deeply resented. They are constantly re-emphasized, both directly by the Western profile in the region, and indirectly through US material support for the state of Israel. Turkey feels particularly uncomfortable with this sustained antipathy towards the West. Turkey is not only formally aligned with the West through its membership of Nato, but its military and political elites identify profoundly with the West. Moreover, an extensive US military presence, both human and material, gives tangible evidence of Turkey's Western alignment. Second only to Israel, Turkey is perceived as an outpost of the Western military alliance willing to serve its collective ends.

Finally, Turkey's three powerful neighbours also share a deep, fundamental suspicion of Turkey itself. Virtually no matter what policies Turkey adopts in the short to medium term, they are unlikely to allay the long-term concerns, even phobias, of its neighbouring states. Chapter 3 suggested that this suspicion emerged from a long and often unhappy historical experience. Not only recent history but political and physical geography and the contemporary political situation would suggest that this attitude is likely to persist.

Relations with Syria

Relations between Syria and Turkey have never been cordial, but have often been cold. Indeed, decision-makers and commentators in Ankara have generally regarded Syria as the most difficult of all Turkey's problematic neighbours. Chapter 3 indicated that there are complex historical reasons for a profound mutual distrust between the Turks and the Syrians, compounded on the Syrian side by a deep-seated sense of dispossession over the loss of the Sanjak of Alexandretta, now known as the Turkish province of Hatay. This loss offends both the pan-Arabist and Greater Syrian ideologues as well as the territorial nationalists – or much of Syria's political elite. The sense of outrage and the resentment against the Turks for taking over the Sanjak is analogous, though obviously less intense, to the reaction to the loss of another part of Greater Syria, namely Palestine. While the restoration of Arab sovereignty to Palestine would be unlikely to contribute towards the re-establishment of Greater Syria, it is at least clear that if Turkey were to relinquish its hold on Hatay, it would revert to Syria. Such a move is highly unlikely. If Hatay were restored to Syrian sovereignty, the Turks fear that it could prove the thin end of an irredentist wedge.[3] Hatay appears to be only a symbol hiding an apparently broader claim to Turkish territory on the part of the Syrian state.

The historical suspicion and the outstanding territorial dispute have in the past been exacerbated by East–West tension, for, as one writer on Turkish–Syrian affairs has put it, 'the frontier between the Eastern and Western blocs ... runs more or less along the Turkish–Syrian border'.[4] It was during the 1950s and the heyday of the Baghdad Pact that the East–West tension was most clearly embodied in relations between Turkey and Syria. Though the tensions of that period which appeared to border on physical conflict have receded, Turkey and Syria have continued to regard one another as being on opposite sides of an essentially bipolar world. This East–West paradigm which has largely determined Turkish–Syrian relations will, presumably, fade with time in a post-bipolar world. However, a marked reduction in the East–West suspicion which overlays local frictions is most unlikely to take place with the same speed as in the European theatre, especially among the Turkish military. The USSR will most likely continue to be Syria's main arms supplier, albeit on a more commercial basis, and Turkey will continue to be wary of its superpower neighbour. In short, the residue of the East–West confrontation will persist between Turkey and Syria for some time to come.

During the 1980s another substantial issue emerged to blight the bilateral relationship: the vexed question of the waters of the Euphrates River. Turkey wishes, as is its right under international law, to use greater volumes of the river to service the irrigation schemes and hydroelectric power projects provided for in the blueprint of GAP. Cognizant of Syrian concerns about repercussions on its own hydroelectric power plants, Turkey guaranteed an average annual minimum flow from the river into Syria. But this has not prevented periodic sub-annual reductions in the flow of the river, as Chapter 8 explains.

Implicit in the Euphrates case, as with all matters of bilateral and trilateral concern, is an even more overriding question: which of the aspiring regional powers is in the ascendant. There can be no doubt that the Euphrates issue is deeply unpalatable to the Syrians because it is Turkey, a perceived regional rival, which has control over the headwaters. No matter what guarantees are given to Syria about the waters, they result from decisions taken solely by the Turks. Syria is concerned because it knows that they can be withdrawn as easily as they were extended.

The imbalance in the water issue does not mean that Syria is without leverage over Turkey. Its main instrument is the support of groups dedicated to violent confrontation with Turkey. Syrian support of fringe leftist groups committed to violence dates from the early 1970s. During the 1980s, Damascus continued this approach by aiding ethnically oriented groups. These have included both Armenian groups, such as the Armenian Secret Army for the Liberation of Armenia (ASALA), and Kurdish groups, notably the PKK. While ASALA and other Armenian groups have largely abandoned armed confrontation, the PKK is more active than ever. For its part Turkey, too, has harboured Syrian émigrés, whose organization, the Muslim Brotherhood, has been responsible for deaths and destruction inside Syria. Such assistance, however, came to an end in 1986, while Syria still persists with its policy of backing Turkish insurgents – a principle which has helped to foster deep-seated antipathy towards Syria in Turkey.

There is no real doubt that Syria gives protection to the PKK insurgents and facilitates their violent tactics. At various times PKK bases have existed inside Syria. There is no doubt whatsoever that PKK bases exist today in the Beqaa Valley in Lebanon. Syria's claim that it has no jurisdiction over this area is unconvincing. In any case, PKK operatives have to cross at least 150 kilometres of Syrian territory to reach the Turkish border. The idea that this would be routinely possible without Syrian complicity is not persuasive. Syria further insists, rather more convincingly, that it is not able to police the whole length of its 900-kilometre border with Turkey, especially in view of the type of terrain involved, and the fact that its military strength is concentrated in the south and in Lebanon.[5] Indeed, by failing to stop the insurgents from entering their country, the Turks give substance to this argument. The Syrian claims of innocence would be more powerful if the acknowledged leader of the PKK, Abdullah Ocalan, did not possess a residence in Damascus, and the PKK did not hold its party congresses in Syria.

Syrian assistance to the PKK, indirect through it may be, has stung Turkey. The Turkish government's response has been to engage the Syrians in a constructive dialogue, repeatedly trying to reach a formal understanding whereby the Syrians end their support for the insurgents. Turkey has attempted to use a range of mostly economic inducements to this end, including help with oil and gas prospecting, the export of electricity, the provision of drinking water by pipeline, greater volumes of formal trade and even loans. Periodically, the Turkish government has obtained Syrian commitments to end aid for the insurgents, and the two countries have signed reciprocal extradition protocols. These accords and understandings have rarely lasted for long, leading to increasing bitterness and recrimination on the Turkish side.

One example will serve to illustrate the mercurial nature of the Turkish–Syrian relationship on this matter and helps explain the deepening Turkish view of the Syrian regime as duplicitous. In July 1987 the then Turkish Prime Minister, Turgut Özal, paid a state visit to Syria. The Turkish side brought up the insurgency problem, while Syria raised the Euphrates water issue. The visit ended with two protocols: on water, Turkey made a guarantee of a minimum average annual flow of 500 cubic metres per second; on security, each side undertook to prevent activities against the other from originating in its territory, and to extradite those responsible. Initially, the PKK training camps in Syria were moved to the Beqaa Valley, though the insurgents continued to pass through Syria to undertake their missions. According to the Turks, those members of the PKK and others captured continued to admit that they had been trained by the Syrian intelligence bureau, the *mukhabarat*. Though the water protocol continued to be observed, by early 1988 the PKK had resumed the use of their camps in Syria.[6]

In 1990, the Turkish authorities became increasingly angry with the Syrian support for the PKK as insurgent activity, and consequent civil unrest among portions of the Kurdish community, intensified.[7] Turkish politicians were increasingly willing to name Syria as the foreign power aiding the insurgents. Sections of the Turkish press even demanded military action against the camps in the Beqaa Valley. The direct military option appeared to be problematic, if only because of Syria's deterrent capability through its well-equipped air force and the quality of its air defence. But if the integrity of the Turkish state is seriously threatened then the Turkish regime, civil and military alike, will examine all its options.

The Turkish elites clearly regard themselves as superior; some even talk of the need to keep an honest dialogue open because of 'the need to civilize' the Syrians.[8] However, there is also considerable nervousness of the Syrian regime, which is seen as politically adept and unscrupulous. On the bilateral front, Damascus is perceived as playing a clever strategic game. Syria knows that it does not at present have the power to wrench concessions from Turkey, so its existing aim is 'to make Turkey weak', in preparation for a time when (as it believes) the broader regional balance, for instance over Lebanon and Israel, will turn in Syria's favour.[9] Syria's surreptitious backing for the PKK is one of its foremost instruments in achieving this weakening of Turkey. The best that can be hoped for in the foreseeable future is that the structural problems which divide the two sides can be managed in such a way as to promote compromise and defuse tension.[10]

Relations with Iran
When the Islamic revolution took place in Iran in 1979 the prospects for bilateral relations with Turkey looked bleak. In many ways Turkey epitomized the sort of state against which the Islamic ideas that came to dominate the revolution were pitted. Turkey seemed to the Islamic revolutionaries to have been a model which the Shah of Iran had attempted to emulate: it was secular, closely allied with the United States, and eagerly adopted Western values and culture. The Shah's father, Reza Shah Pahlavi, had been a great admirer of Atatürk[11] and shared his view that religion was incompatible with progress.[12] Furthermore, Iran and Turkey had entered into two major mutual alliances during this century, the Saadabad Pact and the Baghdad Pact, later reincarnated as the Central Treaty Organization (CENTO). If the relationship between postwar Turkey and Iran had been less than cordial, this was no doubt a subtlety largely lost on Iran's new Islamist leaders.[13]

Though the potential may have existed for real conflict between secular Turkey and the Islamic Republic of Iran it did not take place, first because of some judicious actions by Turkey, and second because of the outbreak of Iran's war with Iraq. Two examples illustrate the former. First, Turkey fully accepted the change of regime in Tehran and was not tempted to intervene in order to determine the outcome of the revolution.

It was to the great credit of the government of Bülent Ecevit that it quickly recognized the new regime in Tehran, despite elements of the Turkish press, for example, which advocated a policy of wait and see.[14]

A second piece of shrewd Turkish diplomacy occurred under Süleyman Demirel's administration, which replaced that of Ecevit. Demirel had deplored the takeover of the US embassy by Iranian students in November 1979. However, he rejected attempts by the United States to persuade its allies, including Turkey, to impose economic sanctions.[15] The Turkish decision was taken with the 1974–8 US arms embargo against Ankara very much in mind. More important was the promise by Iran of extensive economic cooperation. When the war with Iraq began less than a year later, it was extremely useful for Iran already to have punctured the emerging 'ring of isolation'.[16] The war also ensured that the latent antagonisms between Iran and Turkey did not rise to the surface. The increasingly Gulf-oriented nature of the conflict meant that it was the Arab states of the upper Gulf which became involved on a secondary plane rather than Turkey. Once it was clear that the war would not end rapidly, Turkey was far too important as a supply line for Iran to risk pursuing a second ideological conflict. The paradox of close economic links between two ideologically opposed states had been established.

During the war economic interaction between Turkey and Iran greatly increased, as will be seen in Chapter 9. But it was not only in the economic sphere that Iran was willing to court Turkey as a way of securing its neutrality. Iran appreciated the importance to Turkey of the border security question, especially after the launch of the PKK insurgency in 1984. It also did not want to appear less helpful to Turkey in this matter than Iraq had been. In October 1984 Ankara and Baghdad had concluded an agreement which included a 'hot pursuit' clause, thereby rendering it more difficult for the PKK to use Iraqi territory as a sanctuary. The Iranians were generally nervous about this accord as it seemed to indicate growing cooperation between Turkey and Iraq. Tehran wanted to respond positively to Turkey's difficulties, but could not accept the Turkish proposal of a similar accord; the no-go areas established in parts of northern Iraq by the Iraqi Kurdish opposition had no counterparts in Iran. In order to allay Turkish fears, however, Iran did conclude an agreement in November 1984 committing each side to prevent any activity on its territory which threatened the security of the other. It was an accord which was generally enforced, and for the duration of the war there were only a few PKK attacks in Turkey which originated in Iran.

This evaluation is not meant to suggest that the Turkish–Iranian relationship was free from tensions, merely that these were far fewer than might have been predicted in 1979, and that those which did exist were manageable. Certainly, during the war Turkey was one of the chief targets for Iranian subversive broadcasting. There appear to have been good relations between the Tehran regime and the main Islamist party in Turkey.[17] The Iranian political leadership repeatedly demonstrated contempt for the tradition and symbols of the modern Turkish state and, in particular, for the personage of Atatürk. Visiting Iranian dignitaries appeared to relish snubbing Turkish secularism and the memory of Mustafa Kemal. For instance, when the Iranian Prime Minister, Mir Hussain Musavi, visited Turkey in summer 1987 he both refused to visit the Atatürk mausoleum in Ankara – 'a protocol "must" for all visiting dignitaries' – and publicly criticized the philosophy of the founder of the state.[18] Though both the Turkish military and the press took profound offence, the fury aroused by this and other incidents soon dissipated. Such gestures, especially in a country so obsessively proud of its national institutions and its founder, obviously did nothing to foster warmth in what was otherwise a close relationship. However, it did give the radical Islamists in Iran the opportunity to blow off steam without affecting the substance of the bilateral relationship.

Once the ceasefire had become operative in August 1988 and supply routes through the Gulf became more secure, a question mark stood against the future of the Turco-Iranian relationship. Three sets of incidents occurred within a short period which suggested that bilateral relations might indeed have deteriorated. The insults to Turkish national pride appeared not merely to continue but to take on a new intensity. In November 1988 the Iranian embassy refused to follow all the other foreign missions by lowering its flag to half-mast to commemorate the 50th anniversary of Atatürk's death, a refusal which the Turkish daily *Gunaydin* described as 'unforgivable insolence'. In the aftermath of the Salman Rushdie *Satanic Verses* affair the following spring, Iranian insults comparing Turkish President Kenan Evren with Rushdie caused additional offence, especially to the army. The following June, two days after the then Turkish Prime Minister, Turgut Özal, had controversially instructed all flags to be lowered to half-mast as a sign of respect for the recently deceased Ayatollah Khomaini, crowds in Tehran attacked the Turkish embassy.[19]

The intense irritation felt in Ankara at these incidents was aggravated by two more substantive developments around the same time. The first was the 'car boot' saga of November 1988, whereby supporters of the Islamic regime attempted to kidnap a prominent member of the Iranian opposition and to smuggle him back to Iran. The plot was foiled while the man was being driven across Anatolia in the boot of the assailants' car. Members of the Iranian embassy were accused of involvement in the affair. The incident showed that agents of the Iran regime were at large in Turkey, working within the large expatriate community there. Moreover, it indicated that Iran was prepared to use Turkish soil to settle scores with its opponents, and to use members of its diplomatic mission to this end.

A much more serious dispute arose over the so-called 'turban affair'. This was sparked off on 7 March 1989 when the Constitutional Court ruled that the wearing of Islamic headscarves – turbans – by women students on university campuses was illegal. A domestic political tussle then ensued between Turgut Özal backed by the Islamists[20] who opposed the ban on the one hand, and President Evren supported by the army and most of the intelligentsia on the other.[21]

The Iranian regime entered the fray in support of the Islamists, on the grounds that it had a duty to defend the rights of Muslims everywhere.[22] Ayatollah Khomaini denounced the ruling and expressed support for a rash of demonstrations which had been organized by Islamists over the ban. There were suspicions in Turkey that Iranians had helped in the organization and funding of the protests. Marches of support were held in Tehran, and Iranian radio broadcast commentaries critical of the ban. A statement to the Turkish press by the Iranian ambassador to Ankara, Manoushehr Mottaki, suggested that Iran was considering economic sanctions against Turkey.[23] The Turkish ambassador to Iran was then recalled.[24] Ironically, this dispute had erupted just one month after a visit to Turkey by the Iranian premier during which, according to the under-secretary at the Turkish Foreign Ministry, an agreement had been concluded not to interfere in one another's internal affairs.

The firm but belated response by Turkey to Iranian conduct over the turban affair appeared to deter Tehran from further interference. Economic sanctions were not adopted. Ambassadors were restored to both capitals in early June. The controversial Mottaki soon left Ankara, to be replaced by Mohammad Reza Bagheri, a Turkish-speaking Azeri with a public relations touch. Since then, bilateral relations have improved, implying that the events between November 1988 and summer 1989 were an aberration. The death of Khomaini, the election as president of the pragmatic Ali Akbar Hashemi Rafsanjani, the constitutional amendment to establish an executive presidency, and the removal from office of a number of the more uncompromising Islamist radicals could explain the reduction in tension. Iran's exhaustion from conflict and isolation may have acted as an impetus to improve relations on a broad front.

In spite of the pragmatic convergence of interest which has emerged between Turkey and Iran, especially in the economic field, potential difficulties still remain. Three possible areas may be cited: the ideological contradiction which still exists between Iran and Turkey; the large number of Iranian émigrés living in Turkey; and the large ethnically Turkic, Turkish-speaking population in Iran.

Ideologically, Turkey remains a formally secular state and Iran an Islamic state; Turkey is a member of the Western alliance with close links with the United States, while Iran remains firmly wedded to a policy of 'neither East nor West' and has no diplomatic relations with the USA. Furthermore, the formal distribution of power in Iran is still such as to make this ideological contradiction potentially important in policy terms. As long as a major self-conscious centre of radical power, namely the *majlis*, or parliament, continues to exist in Tehran, Iranian policy towards Turkey remains potentially problematic. As other countries have discovered, it is still possible for different state organs in Iran to pursue contradictory aims. In short, the policy of the Islamic Republic of Iran towards Turkey could still be incoherent, contradictory and antagonistic.

No one is sure how many Iranian émigrés there are in Turkey as visas are not required. Estimates differ outlandishly. Some put the figure as low as 250,000,[25] others as high as 1.5 million.[26] A better, though arbitrary, estimate might be 800,000. Either way, it is a substantial figure. The concentration of the émigrés in the cities, in particular Istanbul, and the fact that they tend to be relatively well educated and often prosperous, means that they can potentially exert a disproportionate influence upon Turkish society.[27] While the majority of the émigrés are opponents to some degree of the Islamic regime in Tehran, some of them will be sympathetic to or willing to work with it. On a micro level, Turkey may still be used in future as an arena for conflict between the various groups and factions. On a higher level, the possibility exists that this Iranian community will have a growing impact upon Turkish domestic and foreign policy.

The large ethnically Turkic, Turkish-speaking population in Iran is divided between the Azeris who are Shias, and the much smaller Turcoman community which is Sunni. There is considerable rivalry between the Azeris, particularly those living in the north of the country, and the

Persians. Prior to the advent of the short-lived Pahlavi dynasty, the rulers of Persia were of Azeri stock. At times there has been a strong secessionist current within the Azeris. In the past, Turkey has not competed with Iran as a focus for Azeri allegiance. However, the uncertainty in the Caucasus and the avowedly secessionist position of Azerbaijan vis-à-vis the Soviet state is sure to make Iranian Azeris re-examine their identity.

Turkey is unlikely to want to see fundamental change in Iran. Ankara was concerned about the integrity of the Iranian state in the late 1970s, and welcomed the Islamic republic as a unifying force.[28] Turkey is also unenthusiastic about the prospect of the breakup of the Soviet Union. Such destabilizing developments would be bound to give a fillip to the Kurdish nationalist movement. However, Turkey cannot control events, and may be forced into a reactive posture as change takes place elsewhere. Moreover, Turkey cannot determine whether Tehran is suspicious of a Turanist movement which threatens to loosen the bonds between the Azeris and the Iranian state. If it is, then Tehran may, rightly or wrongly, see the hand of the Turkish state at work.

Relations with Iraq
Of Turkey's three Middle Eastern neighbours it is Iraq with which Ankara has the best potential for balanced relations. This is indeed an irony, given Turkey's role in confronting Iraq during the Gulf crisis. In part, this potential exists for reasons of geography. Iraq is virtually landlocked. Even where it does have an outlet to the sea, its supply lines stretching along the Gulf are long and vulnerable. Baghdad therefore has to depend on second countries for the security of its communications and supply lines. For Iraq, Turkey is the most direct land bridge to Europe. Baghdad's alternatives to extensive dependence upon Turkey are certainly more costly and, even with the experience of the Gulf crisis, arguably more precarious. In return, the potential economic benefits to Turkey of a highly developed trading relationship are extensive, while Iraq has been an important transit route for Turkish exports to the Gulf.

The potential for Iraqi–Turkish cooperation is further enhanced by there being fewer basic obstacles and more convergences of interest than between Syria and Iran. Ankara does not hold territory which Iraq regards as its own. Chapter 3 indicated that Baghdad is still anxious about the continuing Turkish attachment to Mosul, but this has not bred feelings of dispossession and dishonour as in the Syrian case. Unlike Tehran, Baghdad is not ideologically in conflict with the Kemalist philosophies of the Turkish regime. Iraq may have been uncomfortable with Turkey's membership of Nato, but it approves of the secularism of the Kemalist state. The establishment of a regime in Ankara more receptive to Islamist ideas and policy would be perceived negatively in Iraq, which traditionally shows tolerance for its non-Muslim communities.

The main area for a convergence of interest between Ankara and Baghdad, in addition to trade, is their respective Kurdish problems. Of the five states with significant Kurdish populations,[29] Iraq and Turkey have suffered the most from Kurdish rebellion. Indeed, of the five, Iraq and Turkey have the largest Kurdish populations, both absolutely and as a proportion of their total population, and feel most threatened by the problem. This makes them more disposed to help each other and less likely to use the Kurds as an instrument for pressure on each other. The location of the Kurds in Iraq and Turkey, adjacent on the common border, is also important because of the potential threat these recalcitrant groups can pose to communications between the two states.

During the Iran–Iraq war the interdependence of Iraq and Turkey increased markedly, particularly in the economic sphere, where three main areas were affected. In one of these, oil exports, the war deepened a structural interdependence. When the war began there was already one Iraqi pipeline, completed in 1977, which traversed Turkish territory, with a capacity of around 800,000 barrels per day (b/d). It disgorged into the Turkish port of Yumurtalık. However, the closure of Iraq's Gulf terminals in September 1980 necessitated alternative export routes. The deci-sion by Syria in April 1982 to close the Iraqi oil pipeline going across its territory to the Mediterranean brought the Iraqi oil export situation to crisis point.

Iraq responded by attempting to develop export facilities in Turkey and Saudi Arabia. In doing so, Baghdad ignored another neighbour, its close ally Jordan, because an Iraqi oil pipeline to Aqaba would be vulnerable to Israeli attack. The key point is that further enhancing its oil export capability via Turkey, even though or perhaps because it is not an Arab state, was perceived as a relatively secure option by Iraq. The export of crude oil through Turkey was boosted first by the expansion of the capacity of the first pipeline to one million b/d by the end of 1984, then by the construc-tion of a second line, opened in 1987 with a capacity of 500,000 b/d. During the war Iraq also exported considerable volumes of oil via Turkey by tanker truck. This 'moving pipeline' came to an end soon after the ceasefire as Gulf export capacity began to come back on stream. The Turkey pipeline expansion, however, represents an increase in the structural interdependence between the two states.

The closure of its Gulf ports also meant that Iraq had to rely on second countries as conduits for its imports. Iraq maximized its transit routes in order to spread its reliance. Iraqi imports arrived via Kuwait, Saudi Arabia and Jordan as well as Turkey. Nevertheless, the sheer volume of imports, especially in the first two years of the war when Baghdad was pursuing a guns and butter policy, meant that all four states, and Turkey particularly, became important trans-shipment routes. Turkey's location made it the obvious and cheapest route for Iraqi imports from Europe. Moreover, the land link between Turkey and Europe meant that imports could travel by road as well as by sea.

Even at times of acute economic difficulty volumes were vast. In 1986 for instance, when Iraq was suffering in the aftermath of the collapse in the oil price, nearly 4.3 million tonnes in 210,676 trucks were brought into Iraq via Turkey.[30] Direct trade between Turkey and Iraq was also vigorous, with Turkey importing a substantial proportion of its oil requirement from Iraq and making good much of that figure with merchandise exports. During the seven full years of the Iran–Iraq war Turkey imported goods worth $7.93 billion from Iraq and exported to it goods worth $4.88 billion. This made Iraq Turkey's largest trading partner in the Islamic world.[31]

The financial consequences of such large-scale trade represents the third economic factor in the increased interdependence of Turkey and Iraq. The penury of the Iraqi state from 1982 meant that such high levels of Turkish exports could be financed only through credit. As a result, by 1990 Turkey was owed some $2 billion by Iraq.[32] A rescheduling agreement was concluded on the $1.4 billion worth of repayments due in 1989, following some tough negotiations.

Political links between the two states also deepened through common concern over the Kurdish problem. For much of the war, Iraq effectively abandoned large areas of the state in the north to the Kurdish opposition, confining its efforts at control to the strategically important parts of this region. These included the Kurdish city of Sulaimaniya, the oil-producing areas around Kirkuk, the oil pipelines, the main roads in the north and those connecting Iraq with Turkey. This left much of the Kurdish area of northern Iraq as a potential refuge for the PKK. Iraq acknowledged Turkish concerns in this direction. Given the temporary successes of Iraq's own Kurdish opposition, the Kurdish Democratic Party (KDP) and the Patriotic Union of Kurdistan (PUK), Baghdad was reluctant to see Kurdish successes in southeast Turkey. It therefore agreed to a 'hot pursuit' accord in 1984. The Turkish armed forces subsequently made sporadic use of this protocol to keep the PKK on the defensive.

The hot pursuit agreement was not the only way in which Iraq and Turkey cooperated against the Kurdish opposition. In 1984 the Iraqi regime negotiated with the leader of the PUK, Jalal Talebani, in an effort to strike an agreement, apparently hoping to take the pressure off the north through the cooption of one of the two principal Kurdish opposition groups. It seemed that the Iraqi government and the PUK were close to agreement when Turkish Foreign Minister Vahit Halefoğ lu unexpectedly visited Baghdad in October 1984. According to the PUK, the Turkish envoy threatened that an agreement would precipitate Turkey's closing of the oil pipeline and sealing of the border to Iraqi imports.[33] The government–PUK talks broke down almost immediately and the PUK returned to a policy of confrontation. It has never been proved that the Turkish intervention was crucial but Ankara would have had a major interest in preventing any alteration in Iraq's Kurdish policy. Had the accord provided for further autonomy for the PUK-controlled area, then Turkey might have feared the encouragement which it would have given to its own Kurds and the increased isolation it would have suffered over its own, more uncompromising, Kurdish policy.

In fostering this close relationship during the Iran–Iraq war both sides played down areas of potential conflict. The Iraqis were not happy with the utilitarian relationship which Ankara established with Tehran, in spite of the fact that, like much of the rest of the Western world, Turkey tilted in their favour. In criticizing Turco-Iranian ties during the war the Iraqis were careful to dress up their arguments in terms of what was in the best interests of Turkey. The Iraqi regime felt that Ankara should have shown greater fortitude in rejecting both Iranian insults to Turkish national institutions and attempts to interfere in its domestic politics. In view of Turkey's membership of Nato, and the fact that Iran was distracted by the war, the Iraqis believed that Ankara could have been less conciliatory without penalty.[34]

During the war Iraq also soft-pedalled the question of Turkey's increased exploitation of the Euphrates waters for the GAP project. The Iraqis undoubtedly realized that an increased Turkish call on the finite capacity of the river might pose problems for them. Moreover, Baghdad knew and disapproved of the bilateral agreement of 1987, under which Turkey guaranteed Syria a minimum average flow. During the war, however, its objections were comparatively muted, and the fact that the Atatürk Dam was not complete meant that the vexed problem of water rights could be delayed until a less politically sensitive moment.

Restraint was also shown by the Turkish government during the 1980s, especially over the treatment of the large Turcoman population resident in northern Iraq.[35] Ankara had been circumspect in its attitude towards the Iraqi Turcomans even before the war, recognizing their precarious position, given that for Baghdad the Turcomans are a potential fifth column, which could be used to justify the reoccupation of Mosul. A good example of Turkey's attitude towards the Turcomans in Iraq occurred in early 1980. The Iraqi state had decided to execute five members of the community, including a university professor. The Turkish government had tried to stop the executions without publicity, limiting itself to representations 'through diplomatic channels'. Only after the sentences were carried out did the Turkish press get hold of the story. Even so, the Turkish Foreign Minister, Hayrettin Erkmen, was quick to distance Turkey from the affair, saying that it was against international law for one state to interfere in the implementation of the penal laws of another.[36]

The Turkish government maintained this circumspection during the Iran–Iraq war, despite the fact that the position of the Iraqi Turcomans deteriorated. The assimilation process continued (Turkish schools having been closed after the revolution led by Abdul Karim Qasim), and the law prohibiting Iraqis to marry foreigners continued to be applied to Turcomans. The Turcomans felt the ban on foreign travel abroad during the war especially keenly, as they were unable to visit Turkey. It is routinely forgotten that Turcoman (in addition to Kurdish and Christian) villages were demolished in the Iraqi regime's creation of an uninhabited *cordon sanitaire* along the northern border.

In the two years between the end of the war and the start of the Gulf crisis, there were indications that the Turkish–Iraqi relationship would not be as smooth as in the recent past. At the root of this re-emerging uneasiness seemed to be a feeling in Iraq that during the war it had become over-reliant upon Turkey, and now wished to reassert its independence.

Matters of substance have brought out this subtle change. In January 1990 the water issue came strongly to the fore. Turkey's interruption of the flow of the Euphrates was difficult for Baghdad to overlook, since it appeared to reinforce Iraqi dependence on Turkey. A bitter resentment characterized the reaction of many Iraqis. They believed that Turkey would not have taken this action if the war had not significantly weakened Iraq. Baghdad consequently toughened its rhetoric on the water issue later in the year.

On the other side of the coin there was growing unease in Turkey at the qualitative improvements in the weapons at the disposal of Iraq. Along with all of Iraq's neighbours, Turkey has been alarmed at the stockpiling, use and increasing threat of use of non-conventional weapons by Iraq.[37] The development by Iraq during the latter stages of the war with Iran of longer-range missiles raises the prospect that it may be able to hit targets with non-conventional payloads. In theory much of Turkey is now within the range of Iraqi missile capability. The development of such weapons on its borders sharpens Turkey's perception of the Iraqi threat. This has implications for the strategic review which the Turkish armed forces will need to undertake in the context of the expected conventional force reductions in Europe.

Otherwise, Turkey has yet to formulate its reaction to the weapons developments in Iraq. There has been one report, with a photograph, in the Turkish press stating that Turkey has itself developed a new missile. However, expert opinion suggests that this is essentially a battlefield tactical weapon which would be unlikely to carry a chemical payload. The need to project the impression that Turkey has its own modified missile programme seemed to reflect the growing concern over the question among elite circles. The desire to obstruct Iraq's military ambition wherever possible was also clear in Turkey's decision to return parts of the Iraqi 'supergun' to Britain in May 1990.[38] The decision would have been most unlikely during the Iran–Iraq war.

Even on the Kurdish question, where the considerable potential convergence of interest has been noted, there has been evidence of growing difficulties between Turkey and Iraq. The problems for Turkey began almost immediately after the Gulf ceasefire in August 1988. The Iraqi regime turned its attention to its unruly Kurdish population in the north with the intention of re-establishing its authority throughout its territory. In order to do this quickly, the Iraqi armed forces resorted to the use of chemical weapons. As a direct consequence, between 50,000[39] and 60,000 Kurds fled terrified across the border into Turkey.[40]

Ankara was placed in an extremely difficult position by this exodus. On the one hand, it did not wish to appear an accessory to the deed in the eyes of the West, which was critical of Iraq's actions. On the other, it did not want to offend Iraq, with which it has some empathy over the Kurdish threat. Turkey's solution was an uneasy and unconvincing compromise: the Kurds were given refuge in Turkey, but not refugee status. Predictably it brought criticism from both sides. The Iraqis felt that Turkey had trifled with its security in an attempt to curry favour with the United

States and the EC, and to garner votes for Turgut Özal among Turkish Kurds.[41] Having 'infuriated' their neighbours by this policy, the Turks then experienced a 'cooling' in bilateral relations.[42]

Thus the fact that both Turkey and Iraq have a serious Kurdish problem is not sufficient to guarantee good relations or policy harmonization. It is clear that Iraq and Turkey are subject to very different constraints in formulating their response to the Kurdish threat, which is, however, broadly the same in both states. While Iraq has been able to use weapons of mass destruction against its dissident Kurdish population without incurring serious international condemnation, Turkey is more vulnerable to criticism of its policing methods because of its aspirations for full integration into the Western community of states. Nevertheless, the fact that Kurdish opposition is such a threat to both states means that each cannot but be affected by the other's domestic policies on this subject. Ironically, the intensity of the convergence of interest remains a factor capable of bringing the two states into renewed conflict over the practical policies adopted to combat this threat.

6

FOREIGN POLICY PRINCIPLES AND THE GULF CRISIS

Following its unhappy saga of relations with the Middle East in the 1950s, Turkey has steadily developed a series of principles to define and underpin its more recent policy-making on the area. An understanding of these guiding principles makes it possible to comprehend and even to some extent predict Turkish policy towards the region. This chapter will begin by stating these principles, and briefly discussing their background and use.

It is, however, clear that in a changing world, especially one which has altered so profoundly on the cusp of the new decade, there will be modifying pressures on even the most basic principles of foreign policy. Iraq's invasion of Kuwait on 2 August 1990 provided a new challenge to the principles of Turkish policy on the Middle East. The bulk of this chapter will discuss how Turkey responded to this challenge with particular reference to what this tells us about its foreign policy principles. It will end by speculating about the implications of such change and whether they are context-specific aberrations or whether the principles of Turkish policy-making have indeed been redefined.

Foreign policy principles
Ankara has developed its relations towards the region in general with the following seven principles in mind.[1]

(i) *Non-interference in the domestic affairs of the Middle Eastern states.* Turkey has neither the self-confidence nor probably the knowledge to use the personal and kinship dynamics which govern Arab politics for its own gain. In any case, interference in the internal affairs of an Arab state would intensify broader Arab fears of Turkey assuming a neo-Ottoman policy towards the region. Such an action would of course also legitimize interference by Middle East states in the domestic affairs of Turkey, an issue which is highly sensitive given the expansion of unrest in the border areas of the southeast.

(ii) Non-interference in disputes between states in the area. This applies in particular to intra-Arab relations. Again, it indicates Turkey's inexperience and lack of self-confidence in its ability to manipulate such relationships effectively for its own ends. The fear is that Turkey might prove unsuccessful in such a task, even to the point of making Arab states close ranks against a perceived Turkish threat. Turkish neutrality during the Iran–Iraq war indicated the principle's broader applicability and success beyond the realm of intra-Arab relations.

(iii) The development of bilateral relations with all the states in the region. Here the emphasis is on 'bilateral' as well as 'all'. Obviously, the Turkish preference is for these to be developed on a basis of reciprocity and self-interest to ensure both balance and continuity. Implicit here is the desire to bypass the mediation of any supra-national organization, notably the Arab League. This is a throwback to the distrust of the Arab League as a vehicle for radical Arab nationalism in the 1950s and 1960s. A strong Arab League means that the smaller Arab states, such as Jordan, would be less able to pursue an independent foreign policy. Ankara's perception is that this would almost certainly be to the detriment of Turkey.

(iv) Continued fragmentation of the Arab state system. Turkey's historical anxieties about the cohesion of the Arab League also point to the underlying interest of the Turkish state in the continued fragmentation of the Arab state system. The division of the Arab world into a plethora of states has created an important arena of competition within it, serving to undermine its cohesion and so weakening Arab influence on the regional and international stage. The current Arab state system has also had the important function of ensuring that no Arab state is larger or more powerful than Turkey itself. The creation of a supra-Arab state based on Iraq, the Arabian peninsula and Greater Syria, fanciful though that is, would be of immense concern to Turkey because it would combine military power, population and rich natural resources.

(v) The maximization of trade and economic relationships. Since the oil price rises of 1973–4, the Middle East has offered rich economic

pickings. The opportunities for Turkey were increased during the Iran–Iraq war because of its important location. The Turkish economy has benefited enormously from these developments. Though Turkey's Middle East trade profile declined in the late 1980s, it still remains large in nominal terms. The maximization of this potential and the removal of obstacles to it, both economic and political, remains a key objective of the Turkish government.

(vi) The separation of the Middle East from Turkey's role within the Western alliance. In the 1950s, Turkey was regarded by the radical states of the Middle East as Nato's agent, one which saw the region through US eyes. Time and again Turkey sided with Western states in disputes with regional entities, almost regardless of the issues at stake.[2] More than three decades later Turkey is still trying to live down that chapter in its regional relations. Its approach is now more subtle and cautious, but also more tentative. It is keen not to be regarded in any way as doing the West's bidding in the Middle East. National interest now more firmly determines Ankara's policies and actions in the Middle East.

(vii) Scrupulous balance in its approach to the Israel–Palestine question. Turkey has felt that it must steer a careful path between the West and the Arab states with regard to Israel. Ankara recognized the state of Israel less than two months after the United States did in 1949. However, it has been careful to react with greater and more conspicuous sensitivity than the West towards some of Israel's more problematic actions, in deference to the Arab world. At the root of this approach has been a perception, which may now be changing, that the Arab states' policies towards Turkey will be determined to a marked degree by its position on the Arab–Israeli dispute.

Turkey and the Gulf crisis

The Iraqi invasion of Kuwait presented Turkey with some inescapable problems. First, there was the question of the balance of power in the region. By attempting to take over the wealthy and oil-rich emirate, Iraq effectively launched a bid for regional hegemony. Its large and well-equipped armed forces, together with its missile technology and non-conventional weapons capability, rendered this a serious threat. Moreover, the other regional powers were alone incapable of neutralizing Iraq. Israel appeared to have balked at a surgical strike against Iraq during the spring of 1990; Iran was economically, militarily and psychologically weakened by the turmoil of revolution and the eight-year

67

debilitating war with Iraq; Syria was already burdened by Lebanon and the need to maintain vigilance against Israel; the invasion quickly exposed the limits of Saudi armed and diplomatic power. In view of its proximity to the area in general and Iraq in particular, the regional power balance was of critical interest to Turkey. The question was how best to go about curbing Iraqi power without upsetting the precarious balance in other directions.

Second, the geostrategic importance of Turkey in Iraq's supply lines meant that Ankara came under immediate pressure to act against Iraq. Turkey was, together with Saudi Arabia and to a lesser extent Jordan, fundamental to any attempt to impose an economic embargo upon Baghdad. Turkey was significant as an exporter of goods to Iraq and also as a transit point for other goods from third states. Of central importance, however, were the two Iraqi oil pipelines which traversed Turkish territory. Together with Saudi Arabia, Turkey had a crucial role to play if Iraq was to be deprived of its ability to export crude oil.

Third was the question of Turkey's long-term relations with the Middle East and the Arabs in particular. The invasion of Kuwait was so profound a development that Turkey could not remain disinterested. On the other hand, Turkish involvement in such a major regional crisis would inevitably help determine its future relations with the people and states of the region. Turkey could not afford to remain disengaged if the local states were unable to reverse the damage done by the invasion. But direct Turkish involvement on any level would be viewed with great suspicion through much of the region, and might leave it susceptible to charges of neo-Ottomanism.

Fourth, the swift involvement of the United States and certain of its immediate European allies in the crisis meant that Turkey's actions in the context of the crisis would also help to mould its future relations with the West in general and the Americans in particular. Opportunities were likely to present themselves on a series of planes, from the commercial to the diplomatic to the military. More importantly, the very nature of Turkey's short-term relationships with the US and the EC was suddenly opened up to longer-term re-evaluation. The Gulf crisis quickly became an issue involving both the Middle East and the Western relationships of Turkey, and the policies developed by Ankara in the one sphere could not help but have a major impact on the those in the other.

Turkey's initial statements on the invasion were in keeping with the style and substance of its contemporary diplomacy towards the region: they were tentative. Ankara plainly disapproved of the invasion, but felt constrained by the fact that this was a problem between two Arab states, and that the Arabs were strenuously looking for a diplomatic solution to the affair. In other words, Turkey was reluctant to infringe the second foreign policy principle outlined above. Thus the initial pronouncements from the Turkish government were only mildly disparaging, the Anatolian News Agency reporting that Turkey 'regretted Iraq's occupation of Kuwait', and describing it as 'a threat to the maintenance of friendship in the region'.[3]

Turkey was absolved from having to issue tougher political statements by the UN Security Council's prompt adoption of a series of mandatory resolutions. UN Security Council Resolution (SCR) 660, passed on the day of the invasion, condemned Iraq's action and demanded its complete and unconditional withdrawal. Turkey was further given the cover of international legitimacy by SCR 661, passed on 6 August, which prescribed an economic embargo on Iraq, declaring that 'all States shall prevent ... the import into their territories of all commodities and products originating in Iraq or Kuwait exported therefrom after the date of the resolution'. This permitted Turkey to stop all trade with Iraq and to end transit facilities for its oil exports without it being construed as unilateral action.

International legitimacy was, however, not the only factor to be taken into account. There was the possible threat to Turkey resulting from its policy on the export of Iraqi oil, especially via the two pipelines across its territory. As the former British Foreign Secretary, Dr David Owen, wrote, 'Once pipelines are blocked or blown up, a state of war effectively exists between the countries involved.'[4] Turkey also had to bear in mind how its actions would be viewed elsewhere in the region. In particular, it was vulnerable to the recurring accusation of being Nato's arm in the area. The timing and style of policy implementation were, therefore, of great importance.

At first, official Turkish reaction was predictable. On 6 August the influential Islamist Minister of State, Mehmet Keçeciler, who was handling government oil policy, publicly stated that Turkey would not close the two Iraqi pipelines while the one across Saudi Arabia continued to be operational, arguing that Turkey had to give priority to its own needs and interests.[5] This approach was prudent. A unilateral severing of the pipeline through Turkey would be only partially effective if the Saudis did not follow suit; if Riyadh made the first move it would deflect the charge that Turkey was the stooge of the United States in the region. Of course the argument could be and no doubt was made that an earlier move would help the timorous Saudis resolve to cut the Iraqi pipeline across their land. But Turkey would then be going out on a limb, with the attendant risk of acquiring a more negative image in the region.

Around the same time Iraq drastically reduced the flow of its oil through its Turkish pipelines. Mehmet Keçeciler announced that Iraq had shut down one of its trans-Turkey pipelines, while the capacity of the second had been reduced by 70 per cent.[6] Whatever the motives of Baghdad, this should have made it easier for Ankara to delay a complete shutdown until after the Saudi Arabian position became clear. On 7 August Turkey formally banned the loading of Iraqi oil at its Mediterranean pipeline terminals, a decision which David Owen described as 'courageous', and saw as removing the necessity of cutting the pipeline.[7] Keçeciler seemed to agree. As far as he was concerned, Iraq could continue to pump oil through the pipeline until the storage tanks on the Mediterranean ports were full, a process which would, he estimated, take about six days. After that, 'Shutting the pipeline is in Iraq's hands.'[8]

This 'softly softly' approach appeared to be general government policy. Background briefings by the Turkish Ministry of Foreign Affairs to foreign journalists at this time acknowledged that Turkey was dragging its feet over the closure of the pipeline. The briefings emphasized Turkey's need for caution for the sake of its coexistence with the states of the region. Thus did the Minister of Foreign Affairs, Professor Ali Bozer, begin a briefing to diplomatic correspondents on 8 August. In an extraordinary and embarrassing turn of events the briefing was interrupted when a report by the Anatolian News Agency was received announcing that President Özal had decided to close the Iraqi pipelines.[9] The action of the president was quite unexpected in Turkey. The great majority of foreign journalists, foreign diplomats, Turkish politicians and local commentators, in addition to the officials at the Foreign Ministry, appeared to be caught unawares. This general surprise may be explained by the fact that the decision did not accord with the principles underlying Turkish policy towards the region for the past two decades. In particular, the second and sixth of the foreign policy principles outlined above had been infringed. The widespread surprise the announcement caused is further explained by the fact that President Özal evidently wanted to personalize the decision and deliver it with a flourish, as if to emphasize his dominance over national policy-making and his personal commitment to the Western camp.

Two elements appear to have been uppermost in this highly personal decision. First, it seems that President Özal wanted to take the opportunity to bolster what had become a mercurial bilateral relationship with the United States. This was a correct short-term calculation in that it yielded speedy and positive results at the strategic, trade, military, diplomatic and even personal levels. Özal seems to have regarded the crisis as a chance to prove Turkey's strategic regional importance to the USA, a fact which appeared to be enthusiastically acknowledged. On the trade front, one of the first tangible benefits of the crisis was the announcement by the United States in November that it was raising Turkish textile quotas.[10] With regard to the military, Turkey, so badly in need of a qualitative overhaul of hardware, benefited through the supply of $8 billion worth of modern arms, available as a result of disarmament on the Central European stage. These included 1,000 tanks, 700 armoured personnel carriers and a range of missiles.[11] On the diplomatic front, Turkish government officials were clearly under the impression that their chances of being admitted to the EC would be strengthened as a result of the crisis.[12] More crucially, they believed that Washington had committed itself to putting pressure on the EC to help ensure Turkey's admission.[13] An element of vanity may also have been involved. Özal was visibly pleased at the personal attention paid to him by President Bush during the early days of the crisis.[14]

Second, Özal was aware of and agreed with the view of the USA and its immediate allies that Saddam Hussain's Iraq was beyond the pale and that wide-ranging changes had to take place in the northern Gulf if peace and stability were to prosper. There was also deepening concern within Turkey over Iraq's growing military power and willingness to use it.[15] Özal effectively accepted the US and British agenda for the Gulf crisis, which comprised one publicly avowed strategic objective, the full and unconditional withdrawal of Iraq from Kuwait, and an additional hidden agenda, the removal of Saddam Hussain and the neutralization of Iraqi military power, notably its non-conventional weapons. Against such a background it was easier to comprehend why 'Turgut Özal has burnt all his bridges with Saddam.'[16] For Özal the Middle East was in the midst of irreversible change. It was therefore vital for Turkey to be in a position to take full benefit from future opportunities.

The style and substance of President Özal's intervention in the Gulf crisis was, in keeping with the man, a controversial one within Turkey. The initial consensus over the dispute broke down as positions became markedly more polarized. The Kemalist traditionalist elite, which took a more orthodox view of Turkish foreign policy in the region, balked at both the style and substance of Özal's brash partisan action. There was widespread feeling within the establishment that Turkey should have adopted a more neutralist approach, retaining the possibility of playing a mediatory role between Iraq and its immediate adversaries in the region.

Worries then developed over the military role which Turkey might find itself playing in both the short and longer terms. These were raised when an authorization bill was presented to the Turkish parliament giving wide powers to the government, or effectively to the president, to declare war. A number of newspapers warned against participation in any multilateral military action against Iraq.[17] One columnist, Oktay Ekş i, harked back to the past in advising against military action. He wrote, 'If Turkey is provoked into a war with Iraq, Arabs will never forgive her ... just the way they resented Turkey's joining of the Baghdad Pact years ago.'[18] There also appeared to be some trepidation about the sort of role which the Western allies might envisage for Turkey. Deniz Baykal, the deputy head of the SHP, warned that 'Turkey has no need to be the policeman of the region.'[19] Mümtaz Soysal, writing in *Milliyet*, complained that the external danger to Turkey had been exaggerated by forces who want to see Turkey as the policeman of the Middle East.[20]

The cleavage which opened up in Turkey over the Gulf crisis went beyond mere party politics and the reservations of intellectuals. It represented a split dividing President Özal and his supporters from the very bastion of Kemalist traditionalism, the army. The matter came to a head in December 1990 when the chief of the Turkish armed forces, Necip Torumtay, resigned – apparently following a personal snub by President Özal and his cousin, the Defence Minister, who visited the chiefs of the various armed services without him. But the personal tension was a function of differences over Gulf policy, notably the possible use of Turkish military power against Iraq. President Özal seemed to support Washington's plan of early recourse to a military solution, with Turkey figuring in its execution. General Torumtay, together with the military and bureaucratic establishment, appeared to have greater reservations.[21]

A new regional policy orientation?

Has the experience of the Gulf crisis marked a new departure in both principle and style for Turkish foreign policy on the Middle East? The heart of the question is whether Turkish policy during the crisis represents an irreversible, profound change or whether it is more specific to either the crisis itself or the political style and personality of Turgut Özal.

Inevitably, it is too early to establish whether the Turkish stance towards the region more generally has been affected by its policy re-evaluation in the immediate crisis. Much depends on the consequences of the crisis and, most importantly, the postwar security arrangements. It is fair to assume that President Özal has a vision of Turkey's involve-ment in the determination and execution of such security arrangements. By his own admission, the desire to take advantage of whatever changes in the region the crisis ultimately brings was a key factor in his conviction that Ankara should play a proactive and pro-Western role within it. This further suggests that President Özal, who has regularly demonstrated his gift of strategic vision, is unwilling to be tied down by under-lying principles simply because they have been inviolable in the past.

By contrast, much of the Kemalist establishment, whether at the political party, bureaucratic or military levels, has shown itself to be deeply discomforted by Özal the visionary. Their innate caution con-trasts with his apparent impulsiveness; their dourness with his penchant for cutting a dash; their rigorous adherence to carefully defined princi-ples with his flexible pragmatism. It seems that the Kemalist tradition-alist elite is more at ease with the old principles of Turkish regional foreign policy. Indeed, it would seem that there are few men with the strategic vision of an Özal capable of elaborating and implementing a more imaginative and inevitably more risky set of policies. Of course there are those who share Özal's approach, mainly among the Western-educated technocrats in such institutions as the Central Bank, the State Planning Organization and the Under-Secretariat of the Treas-ury and Foreign Trade. By and large, however, they are of a younger generation without the high profile of other political and technocratic figures. It therefore seems likely that if Turgut Özal left the political scene there would be an attempt to reorient Turkish policy towards a more conventional approach. Ultimately, however, the fate of the new approach will in large measure depend upon the legacy of the current president and the changes about to take place in the region.

7

TURKEY AND THE ARAB–ISRAELI CONFLICT

The Arab–Israeli conflict has dominated the politics of the Middle East for four decades. Even the latter stages of the war between Iran and Iraq only briefly eclipsed the Arab–Israeli question as the central preoccupation of the region.

Turkey's policy towards the conflict may be viewed as a metaphor for its uncertainties, ambivalences and contradictions towards the Middle East since World War II. A survey of Turkish government policy in this area since the war shows a number of sudden changes of tack, the majority of them unconnected with changes in the conflict itself. In addition, contradictions have often appeared to exist between the expressed position of the Turkish government and its policy as implemented. By the 1980s, however, Turkey was undoubtedly more successful in adopting even-handed, measured policies which maximized its relationships with all sides, although it was not entirely free from the misconceptions and contradictions which had dogged its policy-making in earlier decades. But its improved diplomatic record appears to have had more to do with changes in external factors than with the self-confidence of Turkish diplomacy towards the conflict.

A historical overview
In November 1947, when the UN General Assembly met to vote on the partition plan for Palestine, Turkey opposed the resolution, a stand consistent with its prewar approach to the Arab territories. It voted against the United States and Soviet Union but with the then handful of

Arab members of the United Nations, and thus shared the crushing defeat suffered by the Arabs. Since the establishment of the Turkish republic its policy had been to support the principle of self-determination, for obvious reasons given the republican struggle against the Treaty of Sèvres.[1] In view of the pronounced Arab majority amounting to some 60 per cent of the population in mandate Palestine in 1947, self-determination would have resulted, one presumes, in the formation of an Arab-dominated unitary state instead of the Jewish state which came into being. The implications of Turkey's policy were therefore clear.

Turkey held to this line immediately after the UN partition resolution, initially refusing to recognize the Jewish state. However, soon after, factors external to the region became primary in determining Turkish policy; from 1949 until 1964 Turkey's alignment with the West was to have a decisive effect upon its regional policy. In particular the urgency of Turkey's need to court the United States in the run-up to the creation of Nato took precedence over the situation on the ground. In March 1949 Turkey was persuaded to recognize the state of Israel. In switching its line, Turkey was able to invoke the changed circumstances arising out of Israel's military successes in the first Arab–Israeli war of 1947–8. The manifest weakness of the Arab regimes made Ankara more confident that it would incur only a negligible penalty from the Arab states. In 1950 Turkey's recognition of Israel was formalized with the appointment of a minister plenipotentiary to Tel Aviv, and in 1952 with the exchange of ambassadors.

The more conciliatory Turkish policy towards Israel, founded as it was on extraneous factors, did not automatically spell a closer bilateral relationship. In the late 1940s and early 1950s the Turkish government displayed considerable suspicion of the formally non-aligned Israel. The existence within Israeli politics of a formidable and varied array of leftist parties was not only unfathomable to the Turkish authorities but also a cause for concern about the long-term political orientation of the Israeli state. This wariness was compounded by a sense of superiority which the ruling Turkish elites had always assumed in relations with the Jews. Although there was no history of persecution of Jews in Turkey, and Turkey had even provided a haven for European Jews fleeing Nazi persecution, the Jewish minority was expected to be loyal and untroublesome in return for protection by the Ottoman and now the Turkish state. The Jews in Turkey were unambiguously regarded by the Turks as being 'timid, passive and compliant'.[2]

The same presumption of superiority characterized the approach of

the Turkish authorities towards Israel. Consequently, Ankara was periodically to resent aspects of the relationship which were incompatible
with this perception, for example the technological superiority of the
Israeli armed forces, and the growing trade imbalance in Israel's favour.
Even against this uncertain background, during the first half of the 1950s
Turkey began to place a growing importance on its emerging relationship
with Israel. This was partly because Israel gradually proved its commitment to confronting international communism, for instance through
its declaration of support for the UN Security Council position in Korea.
Furthermore, Ankara hoped to improve its cooperative but cool relations
with the United States by appealing to American Jewry.

This developing relationship with Israel involved direct costs in
Turkey's relations with the Arabs. In summer 1951, for instance, Turkey
sided with the West in protest against Egypt's decision to prevent the
passage of Israeli ships through the Suez Canal. Although the Turkish
position was sound under international law, it was a blow to Turkish–
Egyptian relations and drew 'bitter criticism' in Egypt.[3] The uneasy relations with Egypt continued after the republican revolution there. In
June 1954 the Turkish Prime Minister, Adnan Menderes, play-ing to the
gallery during a visit to Washington, chided the Arabs by saying it was
time they recognized Israel's right to survive. President Nasser, in a
speech two months later, asserted bluntly, 'Turkey, because of its Israeli
policy, is disliked in the Arab world.'[4]

The establishment of the Menderes government saw a major departure in Turkish foreign policy; instead of ignoring the states to its east and
southeast Turkey sought to bind them into a pro-Western,
anti-communist alliance. Virtually from the beginning of the decade the
Turkish government had sought to develop a security framework including the Arab states. After the failure of the Middle East Command
and Middle East Defence Organization projects Menderes was cautious
about the feasibility of incorporating the Arab states. However, the 'new
look' foreign policy review undertaken by US Secretary of State John
Foster Dulles, which advocated the more strident confrontation of communism and more particularly the organization of a northern tier, caught
the imagination of Menderes.[5] In 1955 this ill-fated policy finally ma-
tured with the establishment of the Baghdad Pact.

In drawing Iraq into this alliance, Turkey was obliged to offer a
number of foreign policy compromises, principally at the expense of
Israel. These included a refusal to issue a declaration of support for
Israeli sovereignty and territorial integrity, and an addendum to the pact

saying that the articles relating to military assistance at times of crisis would be valid within the context of, and indeed were specifically related to, the Palestine problem. Israel's reaction was unequivocal and unconcealed. It frequently indicated its 'resentment'[6] at this pro-Arab policy, whereby Ankara might become an active accessory to military confrontation.[7]

Further signs of this change in orientation came when Turkey, denouncing Israel as 'the greatest threat to peace and order in the Middle East',[8] withdrew its ambassador from Tel Aviv in response to the Israeli invasion of the Sinai Peninsula in 1956. Representation was subsequently downgraded to legation level. In so doing, Turkey was following, in spirit if not in letter, the lead of the United States, which had criticized the trilateral British–French–Israeli action against Egypt, and had obliged the three to relinquish their gains. However, Turkey's action was seen to be 'no more than a gesture which did not mollify the Arabs'.[9] Indeed, the action may have been counterproductive, for it erroneously encouraged Arab opinion to believe that Turkey had realized its initial mistake in recognizing Israel and would be prevailed upon to withdraw it. As events were soon to prove, this was a glaring misconception. A Turkish commentator later observed, 'The indecisiveness of Turkish diplomacy in this regard [Arab–Israeli conflict] has aggravated Arab disenchantment.'[10]

Turkey's policy again appeared to alter in 1958. By this time its Arab policy was in tatters. It was faced by Arab radicalism at its height, and instability rife among the moderate Arab states; its closest ally, the Hashemite regime in Iraq, had just been overthrown. Turkey now lurched in the direction of a strategic relationship with Israel, becoming a signatory to the Israeli-inspired 'periphery pact'. This secret accord was the brain-child of Israeli Prime Minister David Ben-Gurion. He sought to improve and formalize Israel's relations with the countries beyond the 'Arab fence'.[11] Turkey and Iran to the north were included, along with Ethiopia to the south, in an alliance of non-Arab Middle Eastern states. The instability in Syria, Lebanon, Jordan and Iraq facilitated Israel's conclusion of this accord in August 1958.[12] For Turkey, the periphery pact was a symbol of the deep distrust with which it viewed virtually the entire Arab world. In policy terms, it marked the high point of political cooperation with Israel (although formal representation with Tel Aviv was still at legation level).

The demise of Menderes, and the dissipation in the region of the communist threat in general, enabled Turkey to pursue a more relaxed diplomacy from the early 1960s. Indeed, this period marked the beginning of a Turkish Middle Eastern policy capable of maximizing benefits from both sides in the dispute without alienating either. A crucial development was Turkey's experience during the Cyprus crisis of 1964, when the limitations of its friendship with the United States were cruelly exposed, despite its dogged loyalty to Washington throughout the previous decade. Furthermore, it illustrated the isolation of Turkey in the developing world precisely because of its Western-oriented foreign policy. For one writer on the period, the Cyprus crisis 'challenged the basic assumptions upon which Turkish defence and foreign policy had been founded'.[13] Rigid loyalty to the Western camp was no guarantee of securing the national interest. Consequently Turkey's Middle East policy ceased to be a function of its pro-Western alignment and the East–West balance of forces.

Turkey's most successful approach to the Arab–Israel conflict came around the 1967 war and illustrated a 'more independent, flexible, dynamic and diversified approach to the conduct of Turkish foreign policy'.[14] In the run-up to the Six Day War, Turkey displayed understanding of the Egyptian position and refused to join with the group of 'maritime powers' demanding the reopening of the Gulf of Aqaba to Israeli shipping. Following the war, Turkey voted for UN Resolution 242, which prescribed the withdrawal of Israeli forces from territory occupied during the war but asserted the right of all regional states to live within secure and recognized boundaries. This period was one of 'benevolent neutrality', a philosophy which was to serve Turkey well as a model during the longer Iran–Iraq war. One writer has described this era as 'diplomacy at its best', with Turkey being able 'to express sympathies toward the Arab states involved in the [1967] war without offending Israel'.[15]

This policy of benevolent neutrality was nevertheless short-lived. During the 1970s, Turkey routinely supported Arab resolutions at the UN General Assembly, including the November 1975 resolution labelling Zionism a form of racism. Turkey was also increasingly willing to do business with the Palestinian movement. In January 1975 it recognized the Palestine Liberation Organization (PLO) as the exclusive mouthpiece of the Palestinians, even though this was to the detriment of Jordan, a traditionally closer ally of the republic. The impetus for this pronounced pro-Arab and particularly pro-Palestinian tilt was a combination of concern at the effective use of the oil weapon by the Middle Eastern members of Opec, and the commercial opportunities opening up in the oil-producing countries. Turkey's membership of the Islamic Conference Organization in 1976, also in part a by-product of these considerations, further reinforced this bias. In short, the Turkish authorities felt that there was too much at stake economically to risk adopting even a cautiously neutral position. Ultimately, it indicates Turkey's evaluation that its policy towards Israel was fundamental to Turco-Arab relations. In order for these relations to remain cordial and flourishing, the Turkish government made concessions to Arab policy demands.

Such support for the Arabs in general and the PLO in particular continued through and beyond the bilateral peace negotiated between Egypt and Israel. The fact that Egypt, the largest and arguably the most powerful of the Arab states, recognized Israel in 1979 should have made it easier for Ankara to revert to a more balanced relationship between the two sides. However, Egypt's separate peace was struck at a time when oil prices were once again high in the aftermath of the Iranian revolution, and the regional economy had received yet another fillip. The uncompromising response to Egypt's defection by Iraq and Syria, the other principal Arab regional powers, also acted as a deterrent to a more even-handed Turkish policy, especially in view of their geographical proximity. Thus in October 1979 Turkey permitted the PLO to open an office in its capital. Some nine months later Ankara 'vigorously protested' against the Israeli annexation of occupied Jerusalem, withdrawing its chargé d'affaires in Tel Aviv and leaving official representation at the second secretary level.[16]

The extreme swing of the pendulum was again short-lived. Relations between Ankara and Tel Aviv had grown closer once more by the middle of the 1980s. Cooperation in trade and intelligence began to flourish, the latter with respect to the operations of the PKK. As in the late 1950s, the lower level of representation belied the burgeoning relationship between Turkey and Israel from the early 1980s. The atmosphere elsewhere in the Middle East eased the constraints on such ties. The visit of PLO leader Yasser Arafat to Egypt in December 1983 effectively legitimized the establishment of links with Israel. Moreover, the oil price falls of the early to mid 1980s reduced the potential for energy to be used as a political instrument. The decline of the Middle East markets in Turkey's trade profile further eroded the economic leverage of the Arab states. Most importantly perhaps, the Iran–Iraq war, a conflict which came to affect the whole Gulf, increased Turkey's importance to the Arab world and hence widened Ankara's parameters of action.

Contemporary relations

The improvements in Turco-Israeli relations since the early to mid 1980s were arrested with the outbreak of the Palestinian uprising or *intifada* in the occupied territories in December 1987. The uprising refocused Arab and international attention on the plight of the Palestinians.[17] Turkey felt obliged to readjust its position, especially when considerable media attention was paid to the tough measures the Israeli army used to try to suppress the *intifada*.

Despite the increased attention Turkey paid to the predicament of the Palestinians, its relationship with Israel remained intact. Turkey found itself able to pursue an even-handed policy in the area reminiscent of the late 1960s. Turkish national interest certainly dictated that the connection with Israel be continued, especially in combating the PKK and improving Turkey's image in the United States. The changed regional circumstances and, in particular, Egypt's example were very useful to Turkey here. Increasingly in the late 1980s, Cairo managed to combine the peace treaty with Israel, close relations with the PLO and acceptance by other Arab states (it was readmitted to the Arab League in May 1989). Ankara could invoke the example of Egypt as a precedent whenever subjected to criticism by the Arab states for its friendly relations with Israel.

The more optimistic climate for the peace process which emerged between late 1988 and spring 1989 was also propitious. In November 1988, the Palestine National Council (PNC), the PLO parliament in exile, adopted new, more conciliatory political positions. Taken together with clarifications supplied by the PLO leader the following month, they amounted to an acceptance of UN Resolution 242 and the principle of the exchange of land for peace, the renunciation of terrorism, and the implicit recognition of Israel. The fact that the PLO had used the new standing given to it by the uprising to pursue a constructive diplomatic course greatly cheered the international community. Turkey was no exception. It extended full recognition to the state of Palestine (proclaimed at the PNC) on the first day of its existence, becoming the eleventh state to do so, and the first from the Western camp.

Israel expressed disappointment at the speed with which Turkey recognized the Palestinian declaration, rather than at the act itself, presumably accepting it as consistent with Turkey's long-standing position. This entailed acceptance of the PLO as the sole legitimate representative of the Palestinian people, of the right of the Palestinians to self-determination, and of a fuller interpretation of UN Resolution 242 on the question of territory. The recognition of the Palestinian state did not impair Turkey's commitment to the right of all states in the area, including Israel, to live in peace and security. Therefore Israel once again chose to show understanding for the difficulty of the Turkish position. To guard against potential Israeli disaffection, Turkey used the Shamir Plan of May 1989 as an opportunity to make a reciprocal gesture in Israel's favour. Ankara welcomed this plan for elections in the occupied territories as evidence that Israel was interested in keeping up the momentum in the peace process, even if the plan itself was regarded as an evasion in many quarters. In line with its policy of praising all sides in order to alienate none, Turkey further welcomed the Mubarak Plan of autumn 1989 as an attempt to expedite a process which was appearing increasingly to be stalled.

By the end of 1989 it was clear that the peace process was bogged down due to the procrastination of the Israeli government. However, Turkey was spared the need to reconsider its formal position towards Israel by other political events, notably the developments in Eastern Europe which drew media, and increasingly diplomatic, attention away from the Palestine problem. New factors external to the region had thus to be taken into account in Turkey's policy-making on the conflict. The governments of Eastern Europe, which with the exception of Romania had previously shunned Israel, had radically re-evaluated their positions. In rapid succession, Hungary, Czechoslovakia, Poland and Bulgaria established full diplomatic relations with Israel. Subsequently, Greece, which had always conciliated the Arab states as a way of forestalling a Muslim consensus behind Turkey over the Cyprus problem, upgraded its diplomatic links to full relations.

The moves by Bulgaria and Greece perplexed Turkey. Ankara felt that two of its traditional rivals were improving their diplomatic position, with the implication that this could eventually be to the disadvantage of the Turks. Turkey's anxiety was sharpened by the fact that the Balkans were re-emerging as a dynamic sub-system of states, and an unstable one at that. In late spring 1990, Turkey began to talk of restoring its diplomatic representation with Israel to full ambassadorial status. It was typical of the tentativeness in Turkey's Middle East policy that it did not act decisively to present a *fait accompli* to the region, but provided Arab states with the opportunity to apply pressure and shoot down this trial balloon.

Turkey attempted to use the changed international context to promote its relations with Israel in other areas, notably with a scheme to sell drinking water to the Jewish state. This was to be achieved by exploiting Turkey's under-utilized rivers such as the Manavgat. The Ministry of Foreign Affairs was widely reported as stating that a company from the Turkish Republic of Northern Cyprus would handle the commercial side of the operation.[18] The Arab world's immediate disquiet was sharpened by the sensitive nature of the issue, water being both an increasingly scarce resource in the region and the subject of an existing dispute between Turkey and two leading Arab states, Syria and Iraq. Two of the more uncompromising Arab states, Libya and Iraq, retaliated over these proposed water sales. Libya reneged on its promises to service its debt to Turkish contractors, and even held up payments to Turkish workers. Unofficially, Tripoli let it be known that they were 'responding ... to what they see as Turkey's pro-Israeli policy and, in particular, the sale of Turkish water to Israel'.[19] Iraq, for its part, resorted to holding up Turkish lorries at the northern border. Turkey subsequently backtracked on the issue: a statement from the office of the president stated that Turkey would not be exporting drinking water to Israel.

Recurrent factors in Turkish policy-making

In the opinion of a former senior Turkish diplomat, the only country in the Middle East which is 'like us' is Israel.[20] Implicit in this statement is the identification of Israel as a fellow Western country which operates the rules and norms of acceptable international political conduct. Also implied in this short but pregnant phrase is the ambiguous relationship of both Israel and Turkey with Europe; both states share a deep attachment to Europe and European values yet find themselves distanced from the continent of their choice, having to exist in regions where they feel profoundly ill at ease.

The observation also implies that the Arab states cannot be relied upon to operate according to the international rules which have their origin in European history and culture. Ultimately it refers to the fact that both Turkey and Israel are not Arab states, but have to exist in a region where Arab states are more numerous and Arab politics pervasive. Thus Turkey, as a geographically marginal state, and Israel, with its political marginality in the region, regard one another empathetically. Similarly, they both emphasize their distance from the political milieu of the area by identifying with Europe.

Of course, cultural affinity or even political empathy are not the only factors which determine interstate relations. Although the common outlook on the region and the fundamental distrust of Arab politics resulted in the 'periphery pact', this was only one short phase in the 40-year history of bilateral relations.

It has been suggested in the previous sections that two sets of factors – the superpower bipolarity, and then Arab economic power – were dominant in determining Turkish policy towards the Arab–Israeli dispute during the 1950s and 1970s respectively. The 1980s have witnessed changes which would suggest that in future Turkey will not be faced by such monolithic and overwhelming sets of factors when forging its policy on the Arab–Israeli conflict. On the one hand, the old global bipolarity has disappeared, and even the most unreconstructed cold warrior cannot believe that Syria has a hidden communist agenda. On the other hand, the oil markets are generally characterized by weakness. It is difficult to imagine firm oil prices throughout much of the 1990s, despite the experience of the Gulf crisis. In turn, Gulf markets, though still significant, are depressed. This is not to say that commercial issues will not be important in determining policy towards the Middle East. Economic interdependence has deepened through the provision of credit lines by Turkey to such trading partners as Iraq and Libya. But Turkey will not be required as it was in the 1970s to sing a shrill diplomatic tune in order to reap the economic benefits.

Moreover, the old regional bipolar intensity of the Arab–Israeli conflict has been alleviated through the Egyptian–Israeli peace treaty and the recognition given to Israel by the PLO. That is not to underestimate the potential for conflict which still exists, or the enduring need for a formal solution of both the Palestine question and, more widely, the Arab–Israel conflict. However, it does mean that third parties, especially those such as Turkey which are not directly involved, should have the leeway to adopt a more balanced policy.[21] Indeed, if anything, a more mature approach to the problem of peace has been assumed. It is widely regarded by the PLO leadership as a potential advantage for third countries to have a cordial relationship with Israel if this is used to argue for a formal peace settlement on the basis of UN Resolution 242. Such is what Turkey aims to do.

This changed international and regional context means that other factors are likely to be more important in Turkey's regional policy-making. Four main factors will influence Turkey, as follows:

(a) The natural affinity between the Turkish elites and Israel. This will naturally pull Turkey in a pro-Israeli direction, but will be partly

83

balanced by an emotional sympathy which many liberal Turks have for the Palestinians and their plight, especially since the start of the *intifada*.[22] There are parallels between the early years of the Turkish and Palestinian national experiences, although the outcome of the 1921–2 war was very different for Turkey from that of the 1947–8 war for Palestine. There is some sympathy for the Palestinians within elite circles such as the Foreign Ministry, but the prevailing view leans towards Israel, particularly among those with a more strategic perspective on international affairs, who place greater value on past and future Israeli assistance. In turn, a benevolent view of Turkey has traditionally prevailed in Israel. Ben-Gurion, among others of the early Israeli leaders, studied in Turkey. Atatürk is a historical figure who still commands some admiration in Israel.

(b) The assistance which Israel can give Turkey in areas where it enjoys a comparative advantage. This occurs largely through the Jewish lobby in the United States which Israel can mobilize. Attempts made in the early 1950s to help Turkey in this way met with mixed success. While the State Department required little persuading of Ankara's importance, the American press frequently adopted a more negative position, attacking the shortcomings in Turkish democracy.[23] This was in part due to the absence of the strategic relationship which exists today between the United States and Israel; also, historically, the Jewish lobby in America has been pro-Greek.

In the 1980s, assistance to Turkey in Washington met with significantly greater success. Israel was able to divert the Jewish lobby from the Greeks, for example, by persuading it that supporting the Armenian resolution which came before the Senate in February 1990 could help sour Turco-Israeli relations. In addition, the Israeli embassy in Washington was active in ensuring that the resolution failed, for instance by assisting Turkish Jews to travel to Washington to underline the affinity between Israel and Turkey. There was no doubt about the debt which Turkey felt it owed to Israel over this matter. Even four months before the resolution came up for consideration, a senior member of the Turkish Foreign Ministry said his country was 'very grateful' to Israel, the cooperation, in his view, reflecting the maturity of the bilateral relationship.[24] The experience over the Armenian issue has convinced senior figures in Turkey that the pro-Israel network in Washington can indeed deliver the desired results.

(c) The existence of a Turkish Jewish community both within Turkey and within Israel. The Jews in Turkey, concentrated in Istanbul,[25] prob-

ably number around 24,000[26] but are disproportionately influential, owing to the wealth of their community and their prominent position in commercial life ever since the empire.[27] Turkey is likely to be increasingly protective towards its Jewish community because of its influence on the Jewish lobby in the United States, and the continuing sensitivity surrounding the Jewish question in Europe and the America.

The number of Turkish Jews living in Israel is estimated in Turkey at 120,000.[28] Most of them emigrated during the 1960s and 1970s to escape the economic chaos and violence prevailing in Turkey at that time. Their recent arrival means that their Turkish identity is still important to them and they are also very active as a lobby on Turkey's behalf.[29] Turkey has sought to maintain this link as a positive element in the bilateral relationship, in stark contrast to the approach of the Arab states, whose former Jewish inhabitants generally regard them with antipathy.

The Jewish community is also important because of the geographical location of Turkey and its historical importance, ever since World War II, as a conduit for Jews seeking sanctuary in Israel. From then on, Jews fleeing from Iran, Bulgaria, Iraq and Syria have chosen Turkey as a staging post. Over 500 Syrian Jews escaped their country for Turkey during the year up to spring 1990. These migrants are permitted to travel on to Israel.[30] Turkey could become even more important in this respect for Jews leaving the Soviet Union and parts of Eastern Europe, the more so if they arrive as refugees fleeing persecution. However, given the widespread Arab hostility to Soviet Jewish immigration to Israel, Turkey may wish to play down this role and try to avoid becoming a transit point.

(d) The growing potential for commercial links between Turkey and Israel. Trade ties expanded in the late 1980s, in spite of the absence of high-level representation. In 1988 bilateral trade amounted to between $120 million and $130 million. Of this figure, about half was official trade. The remainder was channelled indirectly through a host of front companies located in Europe. Other areas of commercial cooperation are being explored, especially over the buying and selling of water. By 1993 the technology should have been perfected to transport large volumes of up to 20 million tons of water at a time from some of the lesser-used Turkish rivers, like the Manavgat, to second countries. Israel was the first country to show real interest in the scheme.[31] Political difficulties could be finessed by the use of third countries, such as Northern Cyprus, as a staging post in the supply of the water.

There are yet other factors which could be important in the future, but which would *reduce* the potential for ties with Israel. Chief among them is the extent to which Turkey's Islamists can influence foreign policy. The principal independent Islamist group, the Welfare Party, is the only mainstream political party that has radically differed from the government in its foreign affairs priorities. The Welfare Party and other Islamists are active on three issues: against membership of the EC; in favour of closer links with the Islamic world; and against the existing contacts with Israel. The question of relations with Israel is the most specific of the three, and hence is relatively easy to raise as a matter of policy. Moreover, Islamists argue that close relations with Israel preclude closer relations with the Islamic world.[32] Thus, increased influence by the Islamists within Turkish politics may be expected to translate itself into substance with respect to Israel more speedily than with virtually any other foreign policy issue.

8
THE POLITICS OF WATER

Water: a strategic resource

For countries outside the area the Middle East is important as the prime source of oil. Within the region the strategic resource question is viewed rather differently. The problem of securing adequate supplies of water for personal consumption, irrigation and power generation is more pressing. For many of the countries of the area, with their arid territory and burgeoning populations, this problem will be one of growing importance. With the depletion of underground aquifers and the growing salinity and pollution of existing supplies, water will become an increasingly scarce strategic resource in the region. Concern is mounting among commentators that interstate tensions will rise as the region's water supply diminishes.

Against this backdrop, Turkey finds itself in a strategically strong position as the only country in the Middle East which enjoys abundant groundwater resources. The vast majority of the region's rivers and tributaries rise in Turkey, giving it effective control over such resources. In order to exploit its water more effectively, Turkey has embarked upon an ambitious programme which seeks to use its main rivers for irrigation and hydroelectricity. Turkey's riparian neighbours in particular are clearly concerned by its adoption of new policies which will affect their water supplies. Consequently, the plans and activities of the Turks cannot be developed without reference to the consequences for its downstream neighbours. This chapter will examine the question of water and Turkey's interstate relations, focusing on two issues: the Euphrates dispute and associated questions; and Turkey's so-called 'peace pipeline' scheme.

The Euphrates dispute

Background

The most important water resources in southeastern Turkey are the river valleys of the Euphrates (Firat) and the Tigris (Dicle). Both rise in Turkey. Approximately 90 per cent of the water from the 2,800 km-long Euphrates is drained from Turkish territory. A similar proportion drains from Turkey to the upper Tigris, which then flows directly into Iraq at Cizre, before being joined by its eastern tributaries which rise in Iran. After flowing through Turkey, the Euphrates enters Syria at Jarablus, continues for a length of 680 km and enters Iraq at Abu Kamal. In Iraq it combines with the Tigris to form the Shatt al-Arab, which flows into the Persian Gulf. It is this trinity of riparian states which has added to the complexity of the Euphrates issue.

Figures for the discharge of the rivers are imprecise and prone to fluctuation, owing in large part to the inconsistency of the climate and rainfall. The mean average has to be taken over a long period in order accurately to establish the volume of the flow. Statistics also differ according to their source.[1] According to Turkish records based on data taken just upstream from the Syrian border for the years 1937 to 1980 inclusive, the annual flow of the Euphrates into Syria was 30.7 billion cubic metres (cu m). By contrast, the corresponding figure cited by Syrian sources is 28 billion cu m per year.[2]

The use of this long reference period to establish the average flow presents major problems. First, the older the data the more difficult it is to identify recent trends in water flows. Second, the use of the average flow disguises the fact that in individual years the river's water volume can vary markedly. For instance, in 1969 the flow was 86 per cent above the annual average, while four years later it was 62 per cent below.[3] The Tigris annual average flow into Iraq, based on data collected at Cizre from 1946 to 1985 inclusive, is 16.8 billion cu m. Its annual fluctuation is similar to that of the Euphrates.[4]

The Euphrates is Syria's largest river. Within Syria, three main tributaries feed into it: each year the Sajur contributes 125 million cu m, the Balikh 100 million cu m and the Khabur some 1.9 billion cu m.[5] However, estimates diverge wildly over the average annual flow of the Euphrates from Syria into Iraq, ranging between 20 billion cu m and 29 billion cu m.[6]

Syria was the first of the riparian states to try extensively to control the flow of the Euphrates. This reflected its inferior position with regard to water resources, relative to Iraq and particularly Turkey. The Soviet Union was responsible for the construction of the Tabqa or al-Thawra Dam on the Euphrates, 40 miles south of the Turkish border; the filling of Lake Assad, with a total storage capacity of 14.2 billion cu m, began in 1976. The dam was built to serve both the agricultural and energy sectors. The power station attached to it contains eight 100 mw turbines. These have regularly worked well below capacity, sometimes producing only one-third of scheduled output, owing to technical problems and the periodically low levels of water in Lake Assad.[7]

In the late 1970s Turkey followed Syria's lead in trying to exploit the Euphrates for irrigation and hydroelectricity. In 1980 a master plan was produced which linked a number of hydraulic projects, thus paving the way for the large-scale integrated approach of the Southeast Anatolian Project (GAP). The first stage of GAP contains 13 projects which will be realized on the Euphrates and Tigris rivers. According to the Turkish government the first stage will cost $12 billion, and will result in the irrigation of approximately 1.6 million hectares and the generation of 7,513 mw of hydroelectric power.[8] The centrepiece of this scheme is the Atatürk Dam, which will be the fifth largest rock-fill dam in the world and will irrigate an area of 875,000 hectares. The first of the dam's eight turbines is scheduled to begin producing electricity in May 1991.

Disquiet among the other two riparian states as to the scale of GAP led to the formation of a trilateral technical committee in 1980. The agreement by Turkey to take part in such talks indicated that it does not simply regard the Euphrates as a Turkish river but recognizes that Syria and Iraq also have riparian interests in it. By the end of 1989 this committee had met fourteen times but had failed to reach a trilateral agreement on the utilization of the Euphrates waters. Although the talks are three-cornered, Turkey is against a multilateral arrangement, contending that it can have no say over the amount of water Syria releases to Iraq, and that this is not necessarily a function of the volume of water which Turkey releases to Syria. Indeed, attempting to negotiate and then enforce the Syria–Iraq element of a trilateral agreement rings too much to Turkey like becoming embroiled in intra-Arab politics.

A bilateral accord, however, was forged in 1987 between Turkey and Syria. Under this arrangement Turkey undertook to release a minimum of 500 cu m/second across the Syrian border. Damascus interprets this accord as a temporary measure to cover the period of the filling of the Atatürk Dam reservoir, pending the conclusion of a trilateral accord. Once the dam is at full capacity, Damascus would expect average flows to return to between 600 and 700 cu m/sec.[9] Iraq has always objected to the setting of such a low figure, and fears that it will suffer the consequences of reduced flows.

The crisis

The concern and suspicions which had been brewing for ten years over the utilization of the Euphrates water came to a head on 13 January 1990, when the Turkish authorities began to fill the Atatürk Dam reservoir. The river was diverted for one month, resuming its through flow on 12 February 1990. During this time the flow into Syria was vastly reduced, consisting only of water from the three small tributaries, the Göksu, the Araban and the Nizip, which feed the Euphrates south of the dam. Syria and Iraq protested about the harm being done to their economies. Indeed, the dramatic drop in the flow of the river caused a great outcry in the entire Arab world. By the time the normal flow was restored the water issue was cited as a possible future cause of war.[10]

The episode is remarkable for demonstrating an approach by Turkey to two of its neighbours which is quite different from the rest of its Middle East diplomacy over the past twenty years. It marks a break with its usual tentativeness and timidity. This abrasive approach was more characteristic of its diplomacy towards the West, notably the United States, in recent years.

The first example of this firmer approach was Turkey's unilateral announcement prior to the fourteenth meeting of the trilateral technical committee that the river flow would indeed be reduced for one month. Unlike the issue of upgrading relations with Israel the following spring, Ankara had made its calculations on the basis of national interest and then acted decisively in pursuing those objectives. The Turkish authorities presented Syria and Iraq with a *fait accompli*, thereby depriving them of the opportunity to use pressure to oblige Turkey to back off. Turkey then used the technical committee meeting simply as an occasion to release the details of the move, and to claim that it had kept its two neighbours fully informed.

A second example occurred before and during the interruption in the flow. In an emergency mission to Ankara in December 1989, a senior Iraqi envoy tried to persuade the Turks to limit the flow for only two weeks.[11] By the end of the following month both Iraq and Syria had issued 'repeated' calls for the period of interruption to be halved.[12] The Iraqi proposal was on one level attractive because it implicitly recognized Turkey's right to hold back the river for its dam projects, while providing a face-saving compromise for all three parties. The Turkish government, however, refused to make political concessions on what they regarded as a technical issue, even rejecting the suggestion by the Turkish Ministry of Foreign Affairs that the period be shortened by two or three days.[13] In reality the shut-off lasted for the full thirty days.

This uncharacteristic fortitude in Turkey's dealings with its Middle Eastern neighbours was chiefly due to the importance of the issue domestically. The dam projects (of which the Atatürk Dam is the epitome) are central to the Turkish government's initiative to improve the national economy, and in particular to boost economic activity in the rural south and east and thereby alleviate the Kurdish problem. Moreover, the relentless publicity given to the GAP project means that increasingly the reputation of not only the government but even the majority of the mainstream political elite in Turkey is bound up with the completion and success of the programme.

In taking the initiative Turkey was also exploiting the relative weakness of its two downstream neighbours. The calculation in Ankara was presumably that Iraq was in no position to court a military confrontation with its powerful northern neighbour, especially over an issue so central to Turkey's perception of its own strategic interests, having only recently concluded a long and debilitating conflict with Iran. Furthermore, any serious deterioration in relations between Baghdad and Ankara over the water issue might have jeopardized Turkey's role as both an important oil market and a supply route for Iraq.

Syria was similarly distracted. It remains the only 'confrontation' state with the ability or commitment to oppose Israel. Syria also remains deeply involved in Lebanon, and has large parts of its army and intelligence resources tied down there. Furthermore, its economy is even more frail than Iraq's. New military adventures would therefore be extremely unwise.

The tough stance of the Turkish government over the Euphrates was not, however, in substance analogous to its actions towards the Middle East in the late 1950s, when it simply acted according to its own perceived interests, and showed little inclination to understand Arab perceptions. On the water issue, through the regular meetings of the technical commission, Ankara had come to appreciate the interests of its two Arab neighbours, hence could predict their disquiet at the water shut-off. It therefore attempted to address their material concerns before staunching the river.

It did so in two ways. First, in the timing of the operation. The Turkish government selected the winter, when rainfall levels in the northern Middle East, though still erratic, are at their height, and the call on irrigation systems is low relative to the rest of the year. Furthermore, in winter evaporation levels are at their lowest. It was reasoned that the consequent adverse impact on farmers in Syria and Iraq would be kept to the minimum.

Second, Turkey moved to compensate its two downstream neighbours by allowing a larger than usual flow from the Euphrates into Syria from 23 November 1989 until 13 January 1990. This was accomplished by releasing water from two of Turkey's existing dams further upstream, the Keban and Karakaya.

Needless to say, Syria and Iraq were somewhat less impressed by these attempts to take their interests into consideration, but were powerless to stop the diversion of the river's flow. Damascus and Baghdad were obliged to accept the *fait accompli*. The two states confined themselves to condemning the move and to orchestrating a general outcry from the wider Arab world, a task in which they were highly successful. There was a 'furious' reaction from the Arab world, especially its media. According to a Turkish estimate, nearly 400 articles were printed by the Arab press on the issue, the majority of them opposing Turkey. The Arab outcry was as successful as it could be in that the Turkish authorities were taken aback by the extent of the reaction,[14] and hurriedly arranged a delegation which travelled throughout the region to explain the Turkish view to governments and media alike, and correct some of the perceived inaccuracies in the local press reports.

The fact that both Syria and Iraq had only such tactics to resort to and did not confront Turkey indicates their relative weakness and also their understanding of the fundamental importance of the project to Turkey. The successful generation of a unified public response by the Arab world against the unilateral interference with the water network holds out some long-term hope for the two Arab riparian states. The outcry over the issue is a great test for the mettle of the Turkish government and of its new diplomatic style towards its neighbours in the future.

Syrian and Iraqi concerns

The reaction of the Syrians and Iraqis to the diversion of the Euphrates was intensely negative for three reasons. The first was the damage which the shut-off itself was supposed to have done. More serious was the second, namely the prospect of future problems due to further expected shut-offs and ultimately to changes in the volume and nature of the water flow. The third and arguably the most profound was the effect which control over water was likely to have over the power relationship within and among the three states.

Though Turkey had endeavoured to alleviate the difficulties caused to Syria by the diversion of the river, some side-effects were inevitable. Damascus claimed that the area serviced by the river from the border with Turkey at Jarablus south to Lake Assad had been particularly badly hit. The compensatory flow rendered by the Turks was available for storage in the lake. However, the extra water could not be utilized along the 70 km upstream. The Syrians claimed that as a result the environment was damaged along this stretch. In particular, so they claimed, the fall in the depth of the river by more than 3 metres created problems for farmers who need the river to irrigate their winter crops. Damascus also asserted that the lower level of water meant that it was of a poorer quality than normal. This would necessarily restrict its domestic use.[15] Two weeks after the cut-off began, the Syrian Ministry of Irrigation claimed that only one of the eight 100 mw turbines on the Euphrates dam was working, and that this had caused power cuts and electricity rationing.[16]

The Turkish government officially denied both that power cuts had taken place and that some key areas of Syrian agriculture had been damaged.[17] The cries of injury and suffering from the Syrians and the refusal by the Turks to acknowledge any adverse effects were an indication of the diplomatic style of both countries. The refusal by either side to give rhetorical ground in a gesture towards compromise illustrates the difficulties of arranging an equitable understanding between them in matters of substance.

Baghdad also complained about the uselessness of the compensatory flows to parts of the Euphrates which were not subject to control by dams. At 120 km, Iraq had an even longer upstream stretch than Syria on which there were no dams capable of regulating the flow of the river. Agricultural settlements as far as the Qadisiyah Dam at Hadithah could theoretically have been affected. The potential damage could have been costly because of heavy utilization of this part of the country, where the Iraqi phosphates industry is located and the floodplain is exploited for agriculture. The actual repercussions on these sectors of the diversion of the main river were not as serious as they might have been because Syria apparently released compensatory volumes of water from Lake Assad during the cut-off period so as not to exacerbate the problem for Iraq.[18] Damascus wanted to be seen by other Arab countries to be trying to improve its relations with Iraq. In any case, at a time of great uncertainty, owing not least to the reduced assistance of the Soviet Union and the strengthened position of the United States and Israel, it did not want its tense relations with Baghdad to deteriorate further.

Instead, Iraq chose to emphasize the negative medium- and longer-term consequences of Turkey's policy as regards both the quantity and quality of future water flows. The Iraqis and indeed the Syrians are alarmed by the likelihood of further disruptions in the flow of the Euphrates as Turkey continues with the Atatürk Dam scheme. Iraq estimates that it will take some four to five years to complete the filling of the reservoir, assuming an above-average flow. If the level of the river is below average during this period then the time necessary to complete the project would be nearer eight years. The scene is therefore set for a possible eight years of periodic disruptions in river flow leading to further potential problems for the undammed upstream stretches in both Syria and Iraq.

An erratic flow over the next decade could have serious implications, particularly for Syria, which is planning to supplement both its hydro-electric power output and its irrigation potential by the further exploitation of the Euphrates. The Tishrin Dam, upstream from Lake Assad, will hold some 2 billion cu m of water when complete and at full capacity. The adjoining power station will consist of six 105 mw turbines. They are expected to contribute an average 1.6 billion kwh per year. At present Syria irrigates only some 200,000 hectares of land with Euphrates water. With the rising demand for food from a growing population, Syria is planning to expand the irrigated areas between three and four times.[19]

For Iraq, the massive expansion of water utilization by both Turkey and Syria threatens to leave it with a much diminished volume of water from the Euphrates. As with Syria, the threat is to both energy generation and agriculture. Baghdad points out that some 40 per cent of its electricity needs are generated in the Euphrates basin. The depletion of the waters of the 10 billion cu m capacity Qadisiyah Dam reservoir, which is fed by the Euphrates, would disrupt this supply. According to the Iraqi authorities, some 5.5 million of their people are engaged in agriculture in the basin, the Euphrates being far more important than the Tigris for the agricultural sector.[20] The majority of them are Shias from the central and southern provinces of the country. In the 1970s and 1980s the Sunni regime in Baghdad worked hard and successfully to increase the standard of living of its Shias so as to promote their loyalty or at least quiescence. A major reduction in the agricultural output of the region would erode the standard of living of whole communities of Shias, with possible political consequences.

Iraqi agriculture is threatened not just by a reduction in the quantity of water resulting from greater use of the river in the two upstream neighbours. Such intensive utilization of the existing water, especially for irrigation, has also raised Iraqi concerns over its quality, notably its salinity and pollution levels. Much of Iraq's agricultural land, though rich in potential, is blighted by growing salinity. According to the Iraqi authorities higher salinity could jeopardize 40 per cent of the agricultural land in the Euphrates basin and would also gravely damage their industrial installations and water treatment plants for domestic use.

The Iraqis have a broader concern with pollution, fearing quite logically that because greater use is being made of the water upstream it will be increasingly impure as it reaches them. Concern is expressed over the probable rise in the chemicals content, since the level of fertilizers and insecticides is bound to rise as the irrigated water seeps back into the river system. The issue of greater pollution and higher salinity levels could well be the greatest threat of all, and one which cannot be addressed through water-sharing agreements.

As in its attitude towards Syria, the Turkish government appears impervious to Iraqi concerns about the consequences of its GAP policy and argues that Iraq has a second major river, the Tigris, with which ultimately to make good any shortfalls from the Euphrates. The two rivers are already linked by a canal, which indeed holds out some potential for the substitution of Tigris for Euphrates waters in Iraq. However, the Tigris will not satisfy all Iraq's problems. First, there is the question of servicing upstream needs, whether upstream from Hadithah or, in the event of the emasculation of the Qadisiyah Dam, upstream from the link channel. Second, this does not take the pollution factor adequately into account, especially as the Tigris waters are also to be exploited under GAP. Third, with Turkey developing the Tigris there is no guarantee that this river may not be severely depleted at some stage in the future. Fourth, Turkey is on soft ground when it argues that the Euphrates should not be viewed in isolation, but that any consideration of its exploitation must be placed in the wider hydraulic context. If this is the case then it could be argued that because one of the main tributaries of the Tigris rises in the Islamic Republic, Iran should be included in wider negotiations. Indeed, if rivers should not be viewed individually then there is a case for including Turkey's other, less utilized rivers such as the Ceyhan and Seyhan, although these of course do not cross national boundaries.

95

The politics of water

Peace pipeline

With existing water resources being depleted in the Arab world at a time when demand is rising exponentially, Turkey sees commercial possibilities in its own abundance of groundwater. Turgut Özal, a politician with the commercial acumen of a private sector businessman, regards Turkey's water as a marketable commodity, the only problems being the technical ones of engineering and economics: how to transport the water to recipient countries, and how to do so at a price lower than that of purified water from newly built desalination plants. Such priorities reflect an attempt to play down arguably the greatest challenge, namely the political feasibility of such a task.

The scheme drawn up for the transportation of the water involved the construction of pipelines between the water-abundant region of eastern Turkey and potential recipient countries in the Gulf and the Levant. As proof of its commitment to the scheme, the Turkish government has commissioned US consultants Brown and Root to carry out a $2.7 million feasibility study. The Turkish government regarded the technology for transporting and pumping the water huge distances as straightforward compared to, for instance, the gas pipelines of Alaska and Siberia. The economics were perhaps more uncertain. Estimates have differed markedly over the cost of the pipelines. One enterprise has put the likely cost at $21 billion.[21] No doubt, were the pipelines ever to be built, costs would escalate even further. The Turkish government is, however, convinced that with the lifetime of each pipeline estimated at around 50 years, it should be possible to attract international financing.

The pipeline scheme involves the exploitation of two of Turkey's medium-sized eastern rivers, the Ceyhan and Seyhan,[22] which both rise in central-eastern Anatolia and flow into the Mediterranean between Mersin and İskenderun. Each day the two rivers carry approximately 39 million cu m of largely unpolluted, good-quality water. In the future, Turkey plans to exploit for its own purposes some 23 million cu m of this flow, and is prepared to export around 6 million cu m a day to the Arab world.

The Turkish government planned two pipelines (see Table 1). The first and largest, known as the 'Western Pipeline', would run south through Syria and Jordan before finishing up in Mecca. It was envisaged that this pipeline would feed the main population centres along a settlement spine between Aleppo and the Hijaz in Saudi Arabia. It would carry 3.5 million cu m of water per day, with Damascus and Amman being the single largest recipients, taking 600,000 cu m per day each. Israel is formally excluded from benefiting from this scheme. However, it is

Table 1 Turkey's peace pipeline scheme

Western Pipeline		Gulf Pipeline	
Location	Assumed water delivered (cu m/day)	Location	Assumed water delivered (cu m/day)
Turkey	**300,000**	**Kuwait**	**600,000**
Syria		**Saudi Arabia**	
Aleppo	300,000	Jubail	200,000
Hama	100,000	Dammam	200,000
Homs	100,000	Al Khobar	200,000
Damascus	600,000	Hufuf	200,000
	1,100,000		**800,000**
		Bahrain	
		Manama	**200,000**
Jordan		**Qatar**	
Amman	**600,000**	Doha	**100,000**
Saudi Arabia		**UAE**	
Tabuk	100,000	Abu Dhabi	280,000
Medina	300,000	Dubai	160,000
Yanbu	100,000	Sharjah/Ajman	120,000
Jeddah	500,000	Umm Al Quaiwain/	
Mecca	500,000	Ras Al Khaimah/	
	1,500,000	Fujairah	40,000
			600,000
		Oman	
		Muscat	**200,000**
Total	**3,500,000**	**Total**	**2,500,000**

Source: Erol Manisalı (ed.), *Turkey's Place in the Middle East*, p. 70.

believed that private plans do exist for the extension of the network to Israel by way of a spur from Amman. This auxiliary scheme could presumably be made public in the event of a peace treaty between Israel and the Arab states, and could even service a Palestinian state which included the West Bank. The second and smaller 'Gulf Pipeline' would run across to Kuwait and then down the west side of the Gulf as far as Muscat in Oman, feeding five states in the process. With the exception of Kuwait, which would receive 600,000 cu m a day, the Gulf Pipeline would disgorge smaller volumes than the Western Pipeline. Taking the two lines together Saudi Arabia would be the largest single recipient, with 2.3 million cu m per day.

The Turks have dressed the whole scheme up by calling it, somewhat extravagantly, 'the peace pipeline'. The notion behind this is that by the end of the century pressure on water resources will be so acute in the region that conflicts may erupt as states seek to expand and secure their own supplies. The construction of extensive pipelines which supply large volumes of cheap water on a reliable basis, regardless of the season, to all the needy states of the region will, it is argued, lessen the pressures on existing natural water resources, and hence head off any possible conflicts.

Though on paper the grandiose plans have seemed simple and convincing to the Turks, they have not been received with rapture by the supposed beneficiaries. The Arab decision-makers worry, first, that such schemes will increase the dependency of Arab states upon Turkey. Second, there is genuine concern on the part of states located towards the end of the pipelines that states upline would have greater leverage over them. It is a concern which, for example, Jordan and Saudi Arabia would have about Syria on the Western Pipeline route. It is a concern which the smaller emirates in the UAE would have about one another. The list is no doubt extensive. The precedents set by first Syria, then Turkey and Saudi Arabia, in cutting oil pipelines running from Iraq in 1982 and 1990 respectively show that such intervention for political reasons is a very real possibility.

The Turkish riposte is that no one state would dare deliberately to close a line, both because it would itself be deprived of water, and because it would invite the combined wrath of the other recipients together with Turkey. This argument is somewhat shaky. It might be possible for a state to extract water yet prevent it from flowing further down. Disruption of the water supply could take place without a formal closure of the line, for instance through fabricated technical difficulties in pumping. United action could not be assumed; it would depend on the states involved in the dispute and the issues dividing them. Moreover, water would not actually need to be cut off for one state to use notional control of the flow to extract concessions from another downline.

The third area of concern is the vulnerability of the pipelines, especially the Western Pipeline, to sabotage or attack, notably by Israel. The Turks dismiss this as fantastical. They thus betray ignorance of and impatience at the Arab experience at the hands of Israel, which has been repeatedly negative over four decades. Equally important, they fail to appreciate the Arabs' deep anxiety that Israel can do as it pleases in the area. The Turks also argue that Israel would not want to antagonize them by disrupting the pipelines and so causing loss to the Turkish exchequer. While it is true that Israel values its relationship with Ankara, this hardly provides a solid basis for Arab water security.

As we have seen, water is becoming an essential component – both an attribute and a symbol – of political power in the Middle East. In the future it is bound to become the object of increasing competition, and hence increasing friction, between states. Alone in the region, Turkey is blessed with an abundance of good-quality water which is easily accessible. This means it will be unable to turn its back on the struggle for secure water supplies in the region, whether it seeks to play an active role in the Middle East system of states, or becomes more fully integrated into any other community of states. Although Ankara has formally stated that the rivers will not be used as a political weapon, in reality it is difficult to imagine that water will not be used, whether explicitly or implicitly, as a lever of its foreign policy.

9

TURKEY'S ECONOMIC RELATIONS WITH THE MIDDLE EAST

Before the 1970s, Turkey's economic interaction with the Middle East was relatively minor, which meant there were few areas of economic policy seen as mutually beneficial.[1] Turkey's preoccupation with security in the region was the motive force for its uncompromising policies with regard to the Middle East. Whereas flourishing economic relations would have helped to build up personal and institutional ties, adding an extra dimension to the more polarized strategic relationship, the 1950s were characterized by deep mutual suspicion between Turks and Arabs. The absence of extensive economic ties continued during the 1960s, although the political relationship was less tense. A real change occurred only during the 1970s.

Turkey's oil crisis
Following the 1973 oil shock, Turkey's oil bill leapt threefold in four years, to stand at $6 billion in 1977.[2] It suddenly became imperative for Turkey to review its economic strategy in order to take advantage of the new opportunities offered by the greatly enhanced purchasing powers of the Arab oil states. This was particularly important as the soaring cost of oil had caused recession in the oil-importing countries of the West and the Third World.

Turkey, however, was slow to respond to the new potential. In 1973, Turkish exports to the Arab countries stood at just $162 million. By 1977, their value had risen only slightly, even in nominal terms, to $185 million. As a proportion of Turkey's export profile the Arab markets had become even less important during this time, with its share of total exports falling from 12.3 per cent to 10.6 per cent over this four-year period. By contrast, imports from the Arab states had risen steadily, with oil obviously inflating the bill. The value of such imports had increased fivefold during this period, from $207 million in 1973 to $1,078 million in 1977. The trade deficit, which had been a manageable $45 million in 1973, had shot up to $893 million four years later.[3]

There were a number of reasons for the sluggish response of the Turkish economy. Strategically, it had been oriented towards import substitution. Consequently, the export economy remained undervalued and poorly resourced, especially in the manufacturing sector. Indeed, the trend up to 1976 had been for Turkey's terms of trade to deteriorate as imports, though on the low side, exceeded exports. By the mid 1970s, however, the etatist approach had evolved into a mixed economy.[4] The private sector could therefore have developed business with the oil-exporting states. In addition to the macroeconomic constraints of the day, such as a shortage of hard currency and rising domestic inflation, Turkish businessmen were at a disadvantage in the region. Despite Turkey's proximity, there was little history of direct trade. When it came to business contacts or familiarity with trading procedures, or even with local cultural norms, Turkish businessmen were ill prepared. Moreover, Turks were handicapped by their ignorance of the Arabic language and its script.

With the export economy retarded but the oil bill rising, Turkey resorted to borrowing. Flush with the recycled petrodollars paid to the oil producers, the international banking community was only too keen to lend to Turkey. In 1977, Turkey found itself in difficulty over its debt payments, and the IMF had to be called in. It was not until the beginning of the 1980s, however, that adequate readjustment measures were implemented. With the generals' *coup d'état* bringing valuable political stability, Turkey was better placed to exploit the next oil price shock in 1980.

The period of expansion

The first half of the 1980s saw the heyday of economic interaction between Turkey and the oil-rich states of the Middle East. Initially, the boom was led by further dramatic rises in the price of oil in the wake of the 1979 Iranian revolution. In 1980 Turkey's crude oil import bill stood just over $2.6 billion (see Table 2). By 1985, despite reductions in the price, crude oil imports were still costing Turkey some $3.2 billion. Iran,

Table 2 Imported crude oil, foreign currency paid and oil prices

Year	Crude oil imports (million tonnes)	Foreign currency paid ($ million)	Oil price ($/tonne)
1975	9.6	754.2	78.29
1976	11.2	972.4	86.72
1977	11.6	1,121.8	96.22
1978	10.3	1,016.5	98.18
1979	8.1	1,205.3	147.48
1980	10.4	2,610.0	248.81
1981	11.5	3,217.2	277.83
1982	13.9	3,538.1	254.44
1983	14.1	3,137.8	221.67
1984	15.5	3,397.6	217.94
1985	15.5	3,213.7	206.91
1986	16.8	1,799.9	106.75
1987	20.1	2,762.2	137.41
1988	21.7	2,429.9	111.77
1989	18.5	2,455.5	132.13

Source: State Institute of Statistics, Ankara.

Iraq and to a lesser degree Libya were Turkey's three main suppliers of oil during this period. In the five years 1981 to 1985, the cumulative cost of Turkish imports from Iran, Iraq and Libya amounted to $5.3 billion, $6 billion and $3.8 billion respectively, oil representing the overwhelming proportion.

This time, however, the increase in the value of trade did not just show up on the import account (see Tables 3 and 4). The rapid transformation of the Turkish economy at the turn of the decade meant that Turkey increasingly had more than simply primary agricultural goods to export. Greater quantities of manufactured goods, which contain more value added than farm produce, were sold to the region. Inevitably, the direction of the export push was structurally conditioned by the origin of Turkey's imports. A strong imperative existed to claw back some of the individual country trade deficits. The size and proximity of the market were also important factors. On all three counts, the Iranian and Iraqi markets came before all others. Ankara was particularly keen to encourage trade with these two countries, recognizing that there was good business to be done during the Iran–Iraq war which began in 1980. Furthermore, thriving economic ties offered the possibility of helping to stabilize the political relationship with both states during a period of great uncertainty.

102

Table 3 Turkey's exports to the Middle East ($ million)

	1981	1982	1983	1984	1985	1986	1987	1988	Total
Algeria	30.8	125.0	127.4	127.5	109.0	177.6	141.9	184.7	1,023.9
Egypt	72.1	145.0	70.2	140.8	141.0	145.2	138.8	188.9	1,042.0
Iran	233.7	791.1	1,087.7	751.1	1,078.9	564.4	439.7	449.3	5,395.9
Iraq	559.1	610.4	319.6	934.4	961.4	553.3	946.2	1,451.1	6,335.5
Kuwait	71.0	86.9	87.0	105.4	116.0	120.8	247.5	309.2	1,143.8
Libya	441.5	234.6	185.3	142.0	58.8	135.8	140.7	203.7	1,542.4
Saudi Arabia	187.4	357.9	364.7	378.0	430.1	357.6	408.4	477.6	2,961.7
Syria	129.4	63.2	58.9	61.7	55.8	62.1	60.6	56.6	548.3

Sources: IMF Direction of Trade Statistics Yearbook, 1989; SIS Foreign Trade Statistics.

Table 4 Turkey's imports from the Middle East ($ million)

	1981	1982	1983	1984	1985	1986	1987	1988	Total
Algeria	34.2	8.7	76.8	105.3	160.8	31.5	130.9	71.6	619.8
Egypt	2.8	13.1	25.0	4.4	6.9	17.0	12.5	14.1	95.8
Iran	514.2	747.7	1,222.1	1,565.7	1,264.7	221.3	947.9	621.5	7,105.1
Iraq	1,563.7	1,417.6	946.6	926.4	1,136.8	768.7	1,152.5	1,188.7	9,101.0
Kuwait	106.7	92.4	168.5	97.5	98.4	209.0	73.9	52.5	898.9
Libya	789.4	889.6	793.4	658.1	620.8	290.9	306.2	100.2	4,448.6
Saudi Arabia	410.4	494.6	268.8	215.7	226.2	175.7	167.3	113.7	2,072.4
Syria	19.0	14.2	3.3	17.8	16.3	18.8	6.2	1.5	97.1

Sources: IMF Direction of Trade Statistics Yearbook, 1989; SIS Foreign Trade Statistics.

The booming economic relationship with both sides was likely to act as a powerful incentive for both parties to accept Turkey's positive neutrality in the conflict. Not surprisingly, then, Iran and Iraq proved in practice to be Turkey's most lucrative markets during this period. Between 1981 and 1985, cumulative Turkish exports to Iran and Iraq stood at $3.9 billion and $3.4 billion respectively. Exports to Iran, which had fallen from $44 million in 1978 to $12 million in 1979 owing to the economic chaos caused by the revolution, revived to $85 million (2.9% of Turkey's exports) in 1980. Turkey's function as a reliable conduit for goods during the war meant that its exports to Iran shot up to $234 million in 1981, $889 million (or 15%) in 1983 and a high of $1,079 million in 1985. Indeed, in 1982 and 1983 Iran was Turkey's largest single export market, outstripping even West Germany. Although West Germany had regained top spot by the middle of the decade, because of the collapse in the oil price and associated payments problems on the Iranian side, the exports to Iran of $440 million, $546 million and $561 million in 1987, 1988 and 1989 respectively[5] were still healthy compared to their value at the end of the previous decade. Ankara was thus able to cut its trade deficit with Iran, which continued after the revolution to be an important source of Turkish oil imports. Indeed, in 1986, Turkey even posted a visible trade surplus with Iran.[6]

The Middle East region as defined by the IMF (that is, excluding North Africa west of Libya but including Iran and Israel) peaked as a market for Turkish exports in 1982, absorbing goods worth some $2.5 billion, or 44.2 per cent of total exports. The Middle East accounted for over 80 per cent of Turkey's trade with developing countries. But although the value of Turkey's exports to the Middle East had risen to nearly $3.2 billion in 1985, the profile of the region in the country's global exports had slipped to 30.4 per cent as the market in the industrialized countries grew more quickly.

In spite of these blossoming export markets, Turkey still ran heavy trade deficits during this time. Between 1981 and 1985 the cumulative trade deficits with Iran and Iraq were $1.4 billion and $2.6 billion respectively. For Turkey's third main oil supplier, Libya, the deficit was even higher, at $2.7 billion. However, it is not true to say that during this time Turkey was carrying large deficits with all its major trade partners in the region. A notable exception was Saudi Arabia, a secondary supplier of crude oil to Turkey, with which Turkey chalked up a trade surplus of more than $102 million in the five years to the middle of the decade.

Given the volume of Turkey's annual oil imports, it could not hope to balance its trade in the early part of the decade. Turkey's trading advantage, however, showed through with respect to the non-oil Arab states whose economies had been distorted as an indirect result of the oil wealth of their neighbours. Syria and Jordan are examples. While Syrian exports to Turkey were valued at just $70.6 million over the 1981–5 period, Turkish exports to Syria totalled $369 million.[7] Meanwhile, Jordan exported $63.5 million worth of goods to Turkey in return for spendthrift consumption to the tune of $533.9 million.

The expansion in trade between Turkey and the Middle East was not confined to merchandise. One of the most effective ways in which Turkey boosted the flow of foreign currency was through the exportation of its contracting services, and the Turkish labour employed by them. It thus benefited from the poor infrastructure in the oil-exporting countries, milking the enormous resources diverted to improve it.

The larger Turkish contracting companies had begun in the mid 1970s to investigate the potential in the oil-exporting countries. Their first success was in Libya, and this encouraged further involvement in the region. There were 22 Turkish contracting companies in the Middle East in 1978,[8] 113 in 1981 and 242 in 1982. The expansion in this sector levelled out at just over 300 in the mid 1980s.[9]

Again it was the early 1980s that saw the take-off in the profitability of the contracting business. Before 1981, some $3.5 billion worth of contracts had been awarded to Turkish companies. In 1981 alone this figure rose by almost 160 per cent to $9 billion. It was to increase by over $3.5 billion and nearly $1.5 billion in the subsequent two years, before tailing off in the middle of the decade. By 1985, however, this meant that the cumulative worth of contracts awarded to Turkish contracting companies stood at almost $15.5 billion. Throughout this period of expansion, Libya remained by far the largest market, its contracts worth nearly double those of the second largest market, Saudi Arabia. In 1985, the cumulative value of contracts in Libya was $8.7 billion, compared to $4.9 billion for Saudi Arabia and $1.3 billion for Iraq.[10]

The boom resulted in a rapidly rising demand by the contracting service companies for Turkish workers to be employed in the Middle East. During the whole of the 1980s the numbers of new Turkish migrant workers moving to the Middle East states far exceeded those going to other regions, Western Europe included. Even before the exponential rise in contract awards to Turkish companies in 1981, the size of Turkish labour exports was growing markedly. For instance, out of the 28,503 new Turkish emigrants in 1980, 20,733 or 72.7 per cent of these travelled to Arab countries.[11] This meant Libya and Saudi Arabia, which absorbed the entire wave of 1980 emigrants (some 72.8 per cent of whom went to Libya).[12]

By the end of 1980 the total number of Turkish expatriates in the Arab world came to 94,000, with 46,000 in Saudi Arabia, 40,000 in Libya and 8,000 in Iraq. Unlike the profile of Turkish expatriates in Europe, 96.8 per cent of those in the Arab states comprised active workers. Thus there were only some 1,400 accompanying children, while the number of female migrants could be counted in tens. In West Germany, by contrast, active workers made up only just over 40 per cent of the community in 1980.[13] The Turkish expatriates in the Arab states were thus overwhelmingly men who went alone, apparently without any hope or desire of remaining there permanently.

In 1985, the expansion of the Turkish workforce in the Middle East was continuing apace, and was outstripping that of other regions even more markedly. In that year 46,867 Turkish emigrants, or nearly 99 per cent of the total, departed for Arab countries,[14] which by now included Kuwait, Jordan, the UAE and North Yemen. Unaccompanied male workers still comprised the majority. By the end of 1985 there were 207,696 Turkish residents in Arab countries, of whom over 94 per cent were workers. The largest number by far were still to be found in Saudi Arabia, where 160,000 Turks were employed. Other significant expatriate communities were: Libya 28,000; Jordan around 8,400; Iraq over 5,300, and Kuwait 4,200. This meant that in the first six years of the decade the number of Turkish expatriates in the Arab world had increased by over 210 per cent. Altogether nearly 9.1 per cent of all Turkish expatriates were in Arab countries, although a calculation on the basis of Turkish expatriate workers alone brings the figure to 18.3 per cent. In 1985, Saudi Arabia had become the country with the second largest number of Turkish expatriates in the world, after West Germany.

The flow of nationals was not all one way. Increasing numbers from the Middle East came to Turkey as the decade wore on. Altogether 118,413 visited Turkey in 1981. In 1985 this figure had jumped by over 250 per cent to 416,648: the number of Saudi Arabians rose threefold from some 10,229 in 1981 to 32,102 in 1985; the number of Jordanians grew from a 1981 figure of 13,195 to 32,713 in 1986, while the number of Libyans rose from just 2,401 in 1981 to 24,832 in 1985.[15] Unlike the Turks travelling in the opposite direction, such visitors arrived for short periods and mainly as tourists. For instance, of the 31,102 Saudis arriving in 1986, nearly three-quarters stated that their visit was for touristic and recreational purposes.[16] Nearly 96 per cent of them stayed for between one and thirty days.[17]

The most dramatic increase in numbers was by Iranians. In 1981, according to official estimates, 11,286 Iranians arrived in Turkey. This figure increased startlingly in 1984 to 137,641 and 213,753 in 1985, falling back to 141,694 in 1986. Again, all these visitors stayed for short periods, overwhelmingly for touristic purposes. These figures do not include the large numbers of Iranians who moved to Turkey as semi-permanent residents. Driven away primarily for political or economic reasons, this community may number around 800,000. Most Iranian visitors were presumably relatives or friends of these residents.

The trend was uniformally upwards, with one specific exception. The number of Iraqis dropped from 13,876 in 1981 to 7,617 four years later because of restrictions on travel introduced due to war-related economic problems, notably the necessity of conserving foreign currency.

Consolidating the relationship

Oil and oil-related economies could not be expected to continue their expansion and absorption at the same rate as in the late 1970s and early 1980s. By the mid 1980s, much of the planned infrastructure of the Arab economies was in place. It was also unrealistic for the oil price to remain at its post-1979 high. The high price of energy triggered a number of what might be called self-righting mechanisms, which in the end helped bring the price down. These included energy conservation, the development of previously high-cost, non-Opec oilfields and the employment of new alternative energy sources. The decade from 1975 to 1985 may therefore be regarded as a freak period for oil prices, and one which will almost certainly not be repeated in such a sustained fashion.

If the years of expansion of the Turkish–Middle Eastern economic relationship took place under freak circumstances, then some retrenchment in the relationship was only to be expected. However, the negligible economic interaction between Turkey and the area before the 1970s can also be seen as freakish and hence equally unlikely to be repeated. It made little economic sense for there to be no economic relationship between Turkey and its neighbouring region, especially in view of the size of some of their markets. There were two other reasons preventing the two parties from drifting back into economic apathy.

First, changes had taken place in the Turkish economy, making it more complementary to the economies of the Middle East than it had been during the first five decades of the republic. It could no longer be characterized as state-dominated and autarkic, undervaluing trade and with nothing but agricultural goods to export. Turkey in the 1980s was an increasingly self-confident, outward-looking economy with competitive manufactured goods such as textiles to export. Moreover, it had little to fear from competition from Middle East manufacturing. With Turkey still dependent on oil for much of its energy, the potential existed for vigorous if no longer extravagant levels of trade.

Second, Turkish entrepreneurs and state officials were now better versed in the business culture of the Middle East. Contacts and partnerships which had been forged during the early 1980s meant that new ventures could be commenced at lower initial cost and with a greater chance of success.

The downturn in the Arab economies and the consequent shakedown in Turkish–Middle East economic relations came more rapidly than might otherwise have been the case because of the oil price collapse in 1986. This had an instant effect on Turkish trade with the region, the first manifestation being a positive one for the Turkish economy as its oil bill fell by over $1.5 billion (to around $1.8 billion in 1986). In 1985 Turkey's import bill from Iran, Iraq, Libya and Saudi Arabia was well over $3.2 billion, most of which was for oil. A year later it had fallen to just under $1.5 billion.

Just as the steep rise in oil imports in the wake of the Iranian revolution had provided an impetus to export, so the sharp decrease in oil revenues provoked an immediate decline in the purchase of exports by Turkey's oil partners. Thus in 1986 the value of Turkish exports to Iran, Iraq and Saudi Arabia declined by 48 per cent, 42 per cent and 17 per cent respectively. Overall, Turkish exports to the Middle East fell by $864 million, or by over a quarter. Though this was a considerable blow to Turkish exporters, the external economy was boosted by a hitherto rare trade surplus with the region. From a deficit of $238.4 million in 1985, Turkey posted a surplus of $393.8 million.

In the years since 1986, the oil price has partially recovered but without reaching the peaks of the early 1980s, save during the exceptional period of the early part of the Gulf crisis. In 1987 crude oil imports to Turkey cost just under $2.8 billion, a more realistic benchmark for the remainder of the decade. This has regenerated trade but on a more sober level. This process of consolidation has produced a more equitable basis for Turkey's external economy. During the oil boom years, trade deficits were routinely registered. In the late 1980s the trading relationship was

Table 5 Turkey's contracting sector

Country	Value of contracts undertaken by Turkish firms since 1974 ($ million)	Value of work in progress, 1990 ($ million)
Libya	9,935	3,079
Saudi Arabia	4,964	105
Iraq	2,500	1,061
Kuwait	473	506
Jordan	185	67
Iran	171	20
Yemen A.R.	111	—
Total	18,339	4,838

Source: Turkey Confidential, No. 10, June 1990, p. 12.

very much more to the advantage of Turkey. In 1987, after the partial recovery of the oil price, the former gigantic deficits did not return. In that year Turkey still managed to post a surplus of $13 million with the Middle East states. With the expansion of the Turkish export sector, this rose to nearly $1.4 billion in 1988 with the Middle East,[18] and $599 million with the Islamic states.[19] Although in 1989 a trade deficit with the Islamic countries was sustained, it was only around $50 million, and unlikely to put the currency under pressure.

The Middle East remains a significant market for Turkish exports. Of course the Middle East is not and is unlikely to be comparable to the EC, with its larger population and more diverse and sophisticated collective economy. While the EC absorbed nearly 45 per cent of Turkish exports by the late 1980s, the Middle East now accounts for some 30 per cent. Though this is over 25 per cent down on the beginning of the decade, it represents a sustainable level of exports to a market which, if not totally reliable, is at least geographically close.

The economic slowdown of the Middle Eastern economies has also affected Turkey's contracting sector (see Table 5). Indeed, after the reversal of 1986 it has made a much more modest recovery than that which characterized the Turkish export economy. In 1986 the cumulative value of contracts with the Middle East states stood at just under $17 billion.[20] By March 1990, this figure had only risen a further 9 per cent to stand at less than $18.5 billion.[21] There were two main reasons for this. First, as has already been observed, much of the infrastructure of the oil-exporting states, and of those in the region which had profited indirectly from the oil boom, was already in place. Second, the fact that Turkish trade was in surplus with the Middle East economies meant that there was no longer any financial incentive for the contracting sector to redress the visible trade imbalance. Indeed, in some cases, for instance with Libya and to a lesser degree Iraq, extra contracting payments only served to pile up the emerging debt to Turkey.

The recession in the Turkish contracting sector in the Middle East inevitably affected the numbers of Turkish expatriates working in the region. But it did not devastate them. In 1987 the number of Turks in the Arab countries was 151,860, a fall of nearly 27 per cent from its high of 207,696 two years before. The biggest fall was in Saudi Arabia, where the total shrank from 160,000 to 112,000 in two years. Elsewhere the reductions were smaller, with Turkish expatriates in Libya and Iraq down from 28,000 and 5,311 to 22,500 and 3,400 respectively. Curiously, the numbers of Turks moving to work in the Arab world continued at a substantial rate and far exceeded the numbers moving elsewhere, perhaps because although the market had slowed down, especially with regard to new business, there was still a considerable backlog of work. By March 1990 the value of work in progress was placed at close to $4.9 billion.[22]

It has already been noted that the oil producers' lower income levels, together with the eradication of the Turkish trade deficits, meant that it became much more difficult for Middle East oil producers to meet their obligations to Turkey towards the end of the 1980s. Increasingly, Turkey was owed money by countries such as Iraq and Libya, and was obliged to extend credit in order to maintain a trading and contracting relationship. By the end of 1988 the Iraqi debt to Turkey was around $2 billion.[23] At around the same time Turkish contractors were owed some $400 million by Libya.[24] The emergence of Turkey, which itself has heavy foreign debts – owing $37.7 billion (exclusive of military debt) at the end of 1988[25] – as a significant creditor is a costly irony.

The level of economic interaction between Turkey and such countries is likely to depend upon protracted and hard negotiations, the extension of further credit and delicate management by the respective governments. Assuming that this occurs, there seems no reason why trade and contracting should not continue at a consolidated level. There are already signs that this is the case. Libya has intimated that it could give Turkish contractors up to $5 billion worth of new contracts in the future, with payments to be made in oil,[26] although Turkey's actions during the Gulf crisis have provoked further economic penalties from Libya. Patient and lengthy negotiations have taken place to try to get Turkish–Iraqi trade relations over the debt servicing hump of 1989–91, with some success. For instance, in 1989 Iraq paid $600 million in debt service in return for the provision of new credits.[27] The Gulf crisis, needless to say, undermined these painstakingly negotiated understandings, as Iraq announced that it would cease to service its foreign debt. If Turkey was capable of maintaining a vigorous trading relationship with a truculent Iraqi regime even during a time of scarce foreign currency, then there must be cause for qualified optimism should a more solvent economy and cooperative regime emerge in the future.

Credit has also been used creatively in relation to one of Turkey's other big Middle Eastern trading partners, Iran. In early 1990, Ankara agreed to extend a credit line worth $700 million to Iran.[28] Around $300 million is being used to help finance new Turkish exports. The remainder has been allocated to allow contractors to take on new construction work in Iran and thereby, it is hoped, open up a country which has previously yielded only modest rewards to Turkish firms. During the Gulf crisis Turkey also showed how quickly it is now able to exploit potential economic opportunities in the region. The effect of the economic embargo on Iraq was partly alleviated by switching trade to Iran. Turkey benefited directly, as Iran's greater effective demand as a result of higher oil prices enabled it to increase its imports from Turkey. It also benefited indirectly as the higher demand for goods to transit through Turkey enabled the transport sector to reassign many of its trucks which had previously operated into Iraq.

Prospects for the future

Turkey's economic relationship with the leading states of the Middle East has been a volatile one, largely because its basis was acutely distorted, most obviously through the ultimately unsustainably high price of oil. Thus it is only since 1987 that the economic relationship between Turkey and the region has begun to stabilize. What the last years of the 1980s showed is that there is a significant and complementary economic relationship to be had between the two parties – complementary in that Turkey is a large net energy importer, while the oil-exporting states are large net importers of food and manufactured goods. There will inevitably be periodic problems, as there are with any sophisticated economic relationship, but the fundamentals exist for a dynamic partnership, with around one-third of Turkish exports continuing to go to Middle Eastern states.

The relationship might improve even further, depending on factors of a long-term nature. First is the question of where exactly Turkey's long-term economic future lies. The EC Opinion of December 1989 has convinced a number of Turkish politicians and businessmen that the republic will never be admitted as a full member of the Community, a view which has been modified only in part by the importance of Turkey in the Gulf crisis. Ankara will reapply for EC membership in 1993, but its chances are poor. Considerable trading potential will still exist with Europe. However, the customs union proposed in the original Association Agreement with the EC and given a timetable for implementation in the Opinion may be of little benefit to Turkish industry, which will have to face full-blooded competition from a Community private sector rendered leaner by the creation of a Single European Market. Given this uncertain future with the EC, there are signs that Turkish businessmen are re-exploring commercial opportunities in the Middle East. The best prospects are in those countries which combine a large domestic market with hard currency or at least with a hydrocarbon collateral. Once again Iran and Iraq top the list, followed by Saudi Arabia, Syria and the newly unified Yemen state, the last two once their oil potential is properly exploited. Libya, as a traditional market of Turkey's, must also be included.

Second is the likely impact of the GAP project on the export potential of Turkey. Once complete, the scheme is expected to transform agricultural output in the southeast of the country. Its actual performance will depend on many variables. However, the massive expansion in irrigated land is expected to lead to both an increase in output and the introduction of new types of crops. At present, large increases in cotton, sugar beet, vegetables, fodder crops and oil seed are predicted, together with massive surges in the production of wheat and pulses.[29] Given that Turkey is already self-sufficient in agricultural goods, the new output will be produced with export markets in mind. The very location of the GAP area means that the Middle East will be explored as a potential market for the increased agricultural output. The massive food shortfall in most Middle East states compared with demand, aggravated by the current massive population growth, makes the region a prime potential market for such produce. Given the likely timescale of the project, GAP is, however, unlikely to make a major contribution to Turkish trade with the region before the next century.

Third, there is the question of energy economics and how the Middle Eastern producers are likely to fare over the next decade. The latest informed opinion is that at some stage in the future demand for Opec oil and gas will rise, as world demand for energy increases and non-Opec supplies begin to tail off, leading to firmer sustainable prices. Because of the profile of Opec reserves this will mean that the Gulf producers within the cartel – Saudi Arabia, Iran, Iraq and Kuwait – together with Venezuela will become increasingly the key global producers of hydrocarbon-based energy. As a result prices, and revenues, will once again begin to rise. The main uncertainty is when the process will begin. Opinion changes regularly depending on circumstances. Sometime between 1993 and the early years of the next century has been suggested. If the conventional wisdom is correct, effective demand in the oil-producing countries will rise as oil prices rise. This would benefit Turkey, both as a creditor and as a major exporter to the region. It would benefit Turkish contractors as well as exporters because towards the end of the decade the oil producers will have to begin repairing and replacing their ageing infrastructure. It would of course mean the republic paying more for its energy inputs, but provided the rises were not sudden or dramatic this would render the negative side at least manageable.

If any one or a combination of these three possibilities comes about, then a fillip to Turkish economic relations with the region looks likely. While this may not happen in the short to medium term, from about 1995 they could all be realized to varying extents. If so, then Turkish–Middle Eastern economic relations may be expected to grow from the firm foundation laid down at the end of the 1980s and early 1990s.

10
CONCLUSION

Turkey's relations with the Middle East present a number of paradoxes. First, for centuries the Turks of Anatolia and the Arabs of the Middle East were joined together within the same state, yet today there is little understanding between the two peoples. Second, the Turks, the Arabs and the Iranians are members of the same religion, yet many Arabs and Iranians regard the Turks as bad Muslims, while many Turks regard the others as backward because of their fusion of the spiritual and the temporal. Third, the regimes in Damascus and Baghdad are arguably those most similar to Ankara as regards the secularity of the state, yet Turkey's relations with them are among its worst in the region. Fourth, Turkey and Saudi Arabia share the same distrust of Moscow and the same pro-Western stance, yet Riyadh, through its backing for Turkey's Islamists, has probably done the most to subvert the Kemalist nature of the regime. Fifth, in spite of so many fundamental ideological and political problems Turkey has continued to enjoy extensive economic relations with Iran, Iraq, Libya and Saudi Arabia.

Against such a backdrop, it is perhaps hardly surprising that Turkey's approach to the Middle East has been so tentative. Despite four decades or more of coexistence with these independent states, Turkey has not built a solid, reliable, working relationship with any of them. It probably has the most in common with Israel, but the pitfalls of the Palestinian problem and the wider Arab–Israel conflict prevent this commonality from maturing. Turkey shares its foreign policy orientations with Mubarak's Egypt, but while the Turco-Egyptian relationship is promising in form, closer scrutiny betrays an absence of substance. One is left with an abiding impression of a Turkey as much on the periphery and as much an awkward and uneasy actor in the Middle East region as it is in Europe.

Turkey's historical and indeed contemporary experience of the Middle East has therefore been, for the most part, a negative one. The prevailing attitudes of the Turkish people towards their Middle Eastern neighbours have been negative. Stereotypical images persist. The Arabs are seen as inferior, vengeful and untrustworthy. The Iranians are regarded as irrational and quarrelsome. Even the Israelis are resented in some quarters for their assertiveness and technical achievements. These negative images are underpinned by practical experience. Much of Turkey's contact with the region is hampered by policy conflicts. On the few occasions when Turkish decision-makers address the Middle East, it is as a region which presents a range of threats, whether as a hotbed of communism, a sanctuary for murderous terrorists or a breeding-ground of Islamic fundamentalists.

Such crisis-related issues are not the only policy interfaces between Turkey and the region. Turkey has profited from a thriving economic relationship, which is sounder today than it has ever been. Tourism has in some small way demystified both Arabs and Iranians. Yet such positive areas of interaction are not the ones which capture the public imagination or which sell newspapers. New issues in the region have arisen which are regarded as posing yet more threats to the Turkish state: water, non-conventional weapons proliferation and medium-range missiles look set to define a new generation of relations.

If this is the case then the current negative image and lack of substance will persist at a time when relations between Turkey and the Middle East are likely to become more intertwined. Turkey may have intentionally fashioned its large export companies on the Japanese model, but the analogy cannot be extended. Ankara cannot trade and do business with the Middle East and still remain distant from its politics and social trends. Turkey has no choice but to become a more integrated member of the Middle East sub-system of states. Its control of much of the region's water resources and the growing range of the weapons of destruction possessed by others ensure this. Nato's decline and the EC's ambivalence leave it with a diminishing range of options.

The enduring problems of Turkey's relations with the Middle East have to be set against the backdrop of a rapidly changing international order that is likely to affect Turkey more than most states, almost exclusively in a negative sense. With the most unstable part of the USSR so close to its borders, Turkey will have deeper reservations about the changes in the Soviet Union than its Nato partners. More than any other member, it is likely to view a diminution of the alliance's defensive character with dismay.

With respect to Europe, Turkey looks set to fare even worse. It is likely to be overtaken in the race for EC membership by states only recently thought to be without aspirations, such as the EFTA countries and the states of Central Europe. Turkey will be left to stand in the corner indefinitely with its national pride badly bruised. Even the smaller Council of Europe, whose badge of membership Turkey wears with pride, is in danger of becoming marginalized by the more broadly defined Council for Security and Cooperation in Europe (CSCE), which includes the Soviet Union. Turkey's relationship with Europe could become analogous to that of the USSR: a geographically marginal state omitted from the emerging spirit of a new and unified continent.

If Europe becomes increasingly defined by a common mix of Occidental culture and Christianity in a frantic attempt to grasp those few common characteristics which bind it together, then Turkey's exclusion would be more pointed. The view that Turkey is part of the Middle East could, ironically, become more deeply entrenched in Europe, even though it is with that region that its dealings are so acutely uncomfortable.

Against such a difficult and worsening tableau what are Turkey's options? Clearly, its uncertain identity, caught between Islam and secularism, does not permit it to go all out in any direction. It remains immobile both in terms of international alignment and individual self-assertion. Surly isolationism has never offered a refuge, and is now less likely than ever to do so. Turkey has only two viable contexts, though neither is perfect. The first is the Turkish nation. Turkey can seek to develop improved ties with the main centres of the Turkic people, especially in Central Asia, regardless of the degree of sovereignty which they enjoy. In fact, it is already doing so with Soviet Azerbaijan. The emergence of a Turkic commonwealth which looks to Turkey for leadership, as the Commonwealth once looked to Britain, is not a flight of fancy. Divisions exist within the Turkic people, but the one characteristic they share is a desire to orient themselves towards Ankara. If Turkey can keep the relationship on a cultural and political plane, improbable though this might be, it would be spared the major cost of such a relationship, namely a large bill for economic aid.

The second option is the Islamic Conference Organization, within which Turkey enjoys much authority and respect. Its full participation is beyond reasonable objection. Yet as a formally secular state it could never aspire to leadership of the organization, and hence does not challenge the considerable influence of states such as Saudi Arabia. Of course in many respects the ICO is not promising raw material. Its diplomacy failed to prevent war between two of its members, Iran and Iraq. The economies of its members are by and large feeble and undiversified. Yet in an increasingly multilateral world it is a club of not inconsiderable importance. With the collapse of the bipolar world, the Non-Aligned Movement has lost its *raison d' être*. If Europe is to define itself increasingly as a Christian entity, then the ICO is imbued with greater legitimacy as an organization. If such a cleavage does open up between a Christian Europe and a Muslim belt to its south and east, Turkey, with its Muslim faith but secular state, may yet find a credible role for itself as a bridge between two communities.

NOTES

The following abbreviations have been used throughout the Notes:

BBC/SWB/ME	BBC Summary of World Broadcasts, Middle East
EIU	Economist Intelligence Unit (*The Economist*)
MEI	*Middle East International*
TDN	*Turkish Daily News*
TPR	*Turkish Press Review*, produced by Turkish embassy, London.

Chapter 2

1 Lord Kinross, *Atatürk: The Rebirth of a Nation* (London: Weidenfeld & Nicolson, 1964), p. 140.

2 There is a debate over how far the ideas of Mustafa Kemal may be collectively termed an ideology. For example Mahmut Bali Aykan, in his unpublished doctoral thesis 'Ideology and national interest in Turkish foreign policy toward the Muslim world: 1960–87' (University of Virginia, 1987), contends that Kemalism was not an ideology because it was neither universal (being confined to Turkey alone) nor rigid (p. 20). Even though Atatürk opted for a loose body of general ideas, best epitomized by the notion of the 'Six Arrows' of Kemalism, it is clear that he established the body of thought which has intellectually oriented the modern Turkish state since its foundation.

3 See Geoffrey Lewis, *Modern Turkey* (London: Benn, 1974), p. 55; and Bernard Lewis, *The Emergence of Modern Turkey* (Oxford: RIIA/Oxford University Press, 1968), p. 333.

4 Geoffrey Lewis, op. cit., p. 165.

5 David Hotham, *The Turks* (London: John Murray, 1974), p. 178.

6 Ibid., p. 179.

7 Andrew Mango, *Turkey: A Delicately Poised Ally* (Beverly Hills/London:

CSIS Washington Paper No. 28 with Sage, 1975), p. 52.

8 The 1965 census based on language cited in Bernard Lewis, op. cit., pp. 221–2.

9 David Barchard, *Turkey and the West* (London: RIIA/RKP, Chatham House Paper No. 27, 1985), pp. 13, 31.

10 Dankwart A. Rustow, *Turkey: America's Forgotten Ally* (New York: Council on Foreign Relations, 1987), p. 27.

11 Geoffrey Lewis, op. cit., p. 213.

12 Barchard, op. cit., p. 25.

13 Ruth Mandel, 'Turkish headscarves and the "foreigner problem": constructing difference through emblems of identity', in *New German Critique*, Winter 1989, p. 35.

14 Ruth Mandel, 'Shifting centres and emergent identities: Turkey and Germany in the lives of Turkish *Gastarbeiter*', in Dale F. Eickelman and James Piscatori (eds), *Muslim Travellers* (London: Routledge, 1990), p. 166.

15 Ibid., p. 170.

16 Selim Deringil, *Turkish Foreign Policy During the Second World War* (Cambridge: Cambridge University Press, 1989), p. 71.

17 Robert S. Eaton, *Soviet Relations with Greece and Turkey* (Athens: Hellenic Foundation for Defence and Foreign Policy, 1987), p. 7.

18 *Jordan Times*, 24 December 1989.

19 *TPR*, 20 December 1989.

20 Interview with State Department official, 18 April 1989.

21 *New Horizon*, February 1990.

22 *TDN*, 15 February 1990.

23 Mina Toksoz, *Turkey to 1992: Missing Another Chance* (London: EIU Special Report No. 1136, 1988), p. 1.

24 *Newspot*, 11 January 1990.

Chapter 3

1 For a summary of the relationship between Aleppo and Anatolia, for example, see Philip S. Khoury, *Syria and the French Mandate* (Princeton, NJ: Princeton University Press, 1987), pp. 103–5.

2 L. Carl Brown, *International Politics and the Middle East* (London: Tauris, 1984), p. 39.

3 Peter Mansfield, *The Arabs* (London: Penguin, 1983), p. 181.

4 For example, the banning of the Ottoman Arab Fraternity in 1909.

5 Bülent Ali Rıza, 'Foreign policy of Turkey toward the Arab states, 1930–60', unpublished doctoral thesis, St Antony's College, Oxford, p. 17, quoting personal communication with ex–President Bayar.

6 Ömer Kürkçüoğlu, 'Arab and Turkish public opinion attitudes towards

questions of the two nations', *Diş Politika* (Foreign Policy), vol. XII, nos. 1–2, June 1985, p. 26.

7 For example, Professor Dr Halil İnalcık, 'Arab–Turkish relations in historical perspective (1260–1914)', in *Studies on Turkish–Arab Relations* (Istanbul: Foundation for Studies on Turkish–Arab Relations, 1986), p. 155.

8 William S. Haas, *Iran* (New York: Columbia University Press, 1946), p. 27.

9 Cengiz Çandar, 'Turco–Iranian relations', in Professor Erol Manisalı (ed.), *Turkey's Place in the Middle East* (Istanbul: Middle East Business and Banking Publications, 1989), p. 40.

10 Ibid., p. 41.

11 Geoffrey Lewis, *Modern Turkey* (London: Benn, 1974), p. 130.

12 Süha Bölükbaşi, 'Turkey's policies challenged by Iraq and Syria: the Euphrates dispute and the Kurdish question', unpublished paper.

13 For a well–researched discussion of the 'Loss of the Sanjak', see Khoury, op. cit., pp. 494–514.

14 For instance, the respected retired Turkish ambassador and scholar İsmail Soysal states that 'the majority of the population were Turks'. See 'Turkish–Arab diplomatic relations after the Second World War (1945–1986)', in *Studies on Turkish–Arab Relations*, op. cit., p. 250. By contrast, Khoury, op. cit., p. 495, states that Turks formed some 39 per cent of the population in 1936, according to the estimates of the French High Commission. Ethnic Arabs probably formed some 46 per cent, although these were divided confessionally between Alevis (28 per cent), Sunnis (10 per cent) and Arab Christians (8 per cent).

15 Lord Kinross, *Atatürk: The Rebirth of a Nation* (London: Weidenfeld & Nicolson, 1964), p. 482.

16 Nuri Eren, *Turkey Today – And Tomorrow* (London: Pall Mall Press, 1963), p. 238.

17 Quotation taken from Khoury, op. cit., p. 496.

18 Rıza, op. cit., p. 20.

19 For instance, Ömer Kürkçüoğlu states that 'Turco–Syrian relations were constantly haunted by the image of the Hatay question', op. cit., p. 30.

20 For example in early 1954. See Political Summary No. 5, 25 February– 10 March 1954, prepared by the British embassy, Ankara, FO371/112922.

21 Summary of speech delivered by President Bayar on 8 November 1955 and reported by the British embassy, Ankara, FO371/117722. The Turkish prime minister of the day, Adnan Menderes, also referred in similar vein to the existence of a 'Middle East gap' in the collective defence network. See Riza, op. cit., p. 177.

22 Summary of remarks made on foreign affairs at the opening of the Grand National Assembly on 1 November 1955 by President Bayar, contained in a report from the British embassy, Ankara, FO371/117722.

23 Ibid.
24 Annual review of events in Turkey, 1957, prepared by the British embassy, Ankara, FO371/136450, 4 February 1958.
25 Efraim Karsh, *The Soviet Union and Syria* (London: RIIA/Routledge, 1988, Chatham House Paper), p. 3.
26 Ibid.
27 Annual review of events in Turkey, 1957, prepared by the British embassy, Ankara, FO371/136450, 4 February 1958.
28 Annual review of events in Turkey, 1958, prepared by the British embassy, Ankara, FO371/144739, 17 February 1959.
29 Minute from Sir F. Hoyer Miller, Southern Department, FO371/144745, 26 March 1959.
30 For example, see letter from Chancery, the British embassy, Ankara, to Southern Department, FCO, FO371/136456, 26 September 1958.

Chapter 4

1 Quoted in David McDowall, *The Kurds* (London: The Minority Rights Group Report No. 23, 1985), p. 9.
2 *Financial Times*, 24 May 1990.
3 Istanbul Chamber of Commerce, quoted in *TDN*, 25 May 1990.
4 *Guardian*, 3 May 1990.
5 William Hale, *The Political and Economic Development of Modern Turkey* (London: Croom Helm, 1981), pp. 224–5.
6 Ibid.
7 Ibid., p. 259.
8 The Turkish state moved simultaneously against the religious and national identity of the Kurds. On the same day that the Caliphate was abolished, 3 March 1924, the religious fraternities and teaching foundations were banned and Kurdish schools, associations and publications were proscribed.
9 McDowall, op. cit., p. 13.
10 For a brief history of the PKK, see Michael M. Gunter, 'The Kurdish problem in Turkey', *The Middle East Journal*, vol. 42, no. 3, summer 1988, pp. 394–7.
11 Quoted from *The Independent*, 7 April 1990.
12 *Newsweek*, 21 May 1990.
13 The PKK is responsible for 'killing hundreds of women and child relatives of pro–government militiamen' in the southeast, according to *The Independent*, 7 April 1990.
14 Governor Hayri Kozakçioğlu, quoted in *Turkey Confidential*, No. 9, May 1990, p. 3.
15 The lower figure reported in *Newsweek*, 21 May 1990; the higher in a *SHP* report, quoting official sources, published on 15 July 1990. See coverage of

it in the Turkish press. The much higher casualty figures claimed by the Turkish authorities for the insurgents relative to their own losses have caused some disbelief among foreign observers. However, this higher figure can probably be explained by the inclusion of civilian deaths. It is not unusual for Kurds to possess firearms for hunting, especially in the mountainous areas of the country.

16 *The Times*, 4 April 1990.
17 *Guardian*, 3 May 1990.
18 See *Kurdish News*, Issue 3, April 1990, p. 1.
19 *The Independent*, 7 April 1990.
20 Interview with the author, 9 May 1990.
21 For an edited translation of Kararname 413, subsequently revised as Kararname 424, see *Turkey Briefing*, vol. 4, no. 3, June 1990.
22 *Newspot*, 1 February 1990.
23 For instance Süleyman Demirel, during a visit to the southeast in May 1990, stressed that GAP was not just about dams. See *TDN*, 8 May 1990.
24 The conclusion of Michael Field in his special report, *Turkey: Its Economy and Prospects* (London: Committee for Middle East Trade, 1989), p. 41.
25 Mahmut Bali Aykan, 'Ideology and national interest in Turkish foreign policy toward the Muslim world: 1960–87', unpublished doctoral thesis, University of Virginia, 1987, p. 26.
26 Quoted in Lord Kinross, *Atatürk: The Rebirth of a Nation* (London: Weidenfeld & Nicolson, 1964), p. 412.
27 Şerif Mardin, 'Religion and politics in modern Turkey', in James P. Piscatori (ed.), *Islam in the Political Process* (Cambridge: RIIA/Cambridge University Press, 1983), p. 142.
28 There were three great waves of religious reform under Atatürk: in spring 1924 the abolition of the Caliphate, the Ministry of Religious Affairs, the religious schools and the religious courts; in summer 1925 the suppression of the religious brotherhoods, the closure of sacred tombs as places of worship and the abolition of the fez; and in November 1928 the formal introduction of the Latin alphabet.
29 The Democratic Party, set up as a result of this relaxation and very much a Kemalist party, called for the re–establishment of the Faculty of Divinity and religious education in general.
30 To quote Edward Mortimer's pejorative view of the thrust of Atatürk's reforms. See his *Faith and Power* (London: Faber and Faber, 1982), p. 147.
31 David Barchard, 'Muslims, be men not mice', *The Spectator*, 10 February 1990.
32 Ibid.
33 Ibid.
34 Reuter, carried in the *Jordan Times*, 25 March 1989.
35 Interview with Professor Ersin Kalaycıoğlu, 18 May 1989.

36 Mortimer, op. cit., p. 149.
37 Interview with Bülent Ecevit, 24 January 1989.
38 See *TDN*, 18 April 1990.
39 See Chapter 5.
40 Gencay Saylan, author of a book on the Islamic revival, quoted in an Associated Press news analysis of the local elections carried in the *Jordan Times*, 4 April 1989.
41 Interview with an experienced Ankara–based foreign diplomat, 15 November 1990.
42 *Tourism Statistics* (Ankara: Prime Ministry State Institute of Statistics, 1987), p. 38.

Chapter 5

1 Phrase used by the US ambassador to Turkey, Morton I. Abramowitz, addressing the Eleventh Annual Convention of the Assembly of the Turkish–American Association in Washington, DC, and quoted in *TDN*, 18 May 1990.
2 If the four countries are compared by population, GNP and per capita GNP the following figures emerge (*sources*: World Bank Atlas, 1990 [population]; CIA *World Factbook, 1990* [GNP and GDP]):

Country	Population (millions)	GNP (billion $)	Per capita GNP ($)
Iran	50.2	97.6	1,800
Iraq	18.3	35 (est)	1,940
Syria	12.1	18.5*	1,540
Turkey	54.9	75*	1,350

*GDP

3 Turks point, for instance, to a Syrian geography textbook entitled the 'Land of Syria', which contains a map showing the Turkish provinces of Adana, Gaziantep, Şanlıurfa, Diyarbakır and Mardin (in addition to Hatay) as lands occupied by Turks but in reality belonging to Syria. The same textbook also denotes the Euphrates and Tigris rivers as belonging to Syria. See Süha Bölükbaşi, 'Turkey's policies challenged by Iraq and Syria: the Euphrates dispute and the Kurdish question', unpublished paper.
4 Elizabeth Picard, 'The present situation in Syria and Turco–Syrian relations', in Erol Manisalı (ed.), *Turkey's Place in the Middle East* (Istanbul: Middle East Business and Banking Publications, 1989), p. 33.
5 For example, see the statement of the then Syrian Prime Minister, Abdul Rauf al–Kasim, in *Hurriyet,* 3 March 1986, and in Bölükbaşi, op. cit., p. 34.
6 *Milliyet*, 11 April 1988, quoted in Bölükbaşi, op. cit., p. 44.
7 For instance, following the 'deadliest raid by Kurdish guerrillas in two

years' the Turkish Foreign Ministry spokesman, Murat Sungar, said that at an imminent meeting of the foreign ministers from both states Turkey would 'bring [frontier] security to the talks with *priority* and *detail*' (emphasis added). See Reuter's report, reproduced in the *Jordan Times*, 14 June 1990.

8 Interview with senior member of Turkish bureaucracy, 19 October 1989.
9 Interview with senior member of Turkish Ministry of Foreign Affairs, 7 May 1990.
10 For all the difficulties, the two sides have managed potentially emotive problems in the past. Note, for example, the case of the shooting down of a Turkish civilian survey plane by two Syrian MiG–21s with the death of the five people on board in October 1989.
11 In fact Turkey was the destination of Reza Shah's first foreign trip as head of state.
12 William S. Haas, *Iran* (New York: Columbia University Press, 1946), p. 153.
13 The Shah was envious of Turkey's privileged position within the Western alliance, while Ankara was nervous and resentful of Tehran's ambitions to become the most powerful state in the region.
14 For instance *Milliyet*, 13 February 1979, quoted in Süha Bölükbaşi, 'Turkey copes with revolutionary Iran', *Journal of South Asian and Middle Eastern Studies*, vol. 13, nos. 1, 2, Fall/Winter 1989, p. 96.
15 For an example of the Turkish rejection of economic sanctions, see the statement by Turkish Foreign Minister Hayrettin Erkmen in BBC/SWB/ME, 25 January 1980.
16 Cengiz Çandar, 'Turco–Iranian relations', in Manisalı (ed.), op. cit., p. 45.
17 Erbakan, the leader of the National Salvation Party, had welcomed the Khomaini revolution because it had freed Iran from 'servitude to America'.
18 Ken Mackenzie, 'Özal vs. the generals', *MEI*, no. 304, 11 July 1987, p. 14.
19 Ken Mackenzie, 'Flag fuss', *MEI*, no. 353, 23 June 1989, p. 13.
20 Professor Erbakan, for instance, claimed that the wearing of the turban was 'the birthright of Turkish women'. See BBC/SWB/ME, 17 March 1989.
21 Ken Mackenzie, 'Islamic dilemmas', *MEI*, no. 346, 17 March 1989, p. 10. The controversy was eventually resolved by allowing individual university presidents to decide.
22 Even at the end of the crisis the Iranian Deputy Foreign Minister, Ali Muhammad Besharati, reiterated this principle. See *Iran Focus*, July 1989.
23 According to *Iran Focus*, July 1989, he threatened that trade would be cut from $2 billion to $400 million in 1989.
24 Associated Press news analysis printed in the *Jordan Times* under the headline 'Turkey recalls envoy to Tehran for consultation', 4 April 1989.
25 US State Department briefing, 7 February 1989.
26 For example, the *Guardian*, 11 November 1988.

27 One commentator estimates that there are one million Iranians living in Turkey, of whom some 400,000 are resident in Istanbul. See Christine Moss Helms, 'Turkey's policy toward the Middle East: strength through neutrality', *Middle East Insight*, Fall 1988, p. 45.

28 See, for instance, the statement made by the Turkish Minister of Foreign Affairs, Hayrettin Erkmen, in which he asserted that the preservation of Iran's territorial integrity was of the utmost importance for the region. BBC/SWB/ME, 25 January 1980.

29 The Soviet Union is the fifth, in addition to Turkey, Iraq, Syria and Iran.

30 Interview with the Iraqi Minister of Transport, Hamad Hamza al–Zubaidi, 11 June 1989.

31 See Union of the Chambers of Commerce, Industry, Maritime Trade and Commodity Exchanges of Turkey, *Economic Report*, 1988, p. 180.

32 EIU, *Turkey on Trial*, Special Report No. 2023, January 1990, p. 35.

33 David McDowall, *The Kurds* (London: The Minority Rights Group Report No. 23, 1985), p. 25.

34 Interview with senior Iraqi official, 10 June 1989.

35 The size of the Iraqi Turcoman population is unknown. According to Kamran İnan, currently a Minister of State in the government, they number around 1.5 million. Anatolia News Agency, 13 January 1987 quoted in Bölükbaşi, 'Turkey's policies', op. cit., p. 37.

36 BBC/SWB/ME, 26 February 1980. In recognition of Turkey's sensitivity over the matter Iraq has permitted Ankara to maintain a Consulate–General in Mosul, to deal with problems arising from the large volume of trade across the common border.

37 The Iraqi military has used chemical weapons against its own Kurdish population. For a discussion of Iraq's non–conventional capability before the Gulf crisis in 1991, see W. Seth Carus, *The Genie Unleashed: Iraq's Chemical and Biological Weapons Production* (Washington Institute Policy Papers No. 14, 1989).

38 See BBC/SWB/ME, 9 May 1990, for the official anouncement by the Turkish Ministry of Foreign Affairs.

39 *Financial Times*, 20 July 1989.

40 Ken Mackenzie, 'Turkey, Iraq and Kurds', *MEI*, no. 334, 23 September 1988, p. 10.

41 Interview with senior Iraqi official, 10 June 1989.

42 *The Independent*, 18 November 1988.

Chapter 6

1 For a Turkish perspective on the major principles governing Turkey's Middle East policy, see Seyfi Taşhan, 'Contemporary Turkish policies in the Middle East: prospects and constraints', in *Diş Politika* (Foreign Policy),

vol. XII, nos. 1–2, June 1985.

2 For example, Turkey sided with France at the UN in 1952 against attempts by Tunisian nationalists to gain independence for their country, in spite of the momentum and widespread support for decolonization among the community of states.

3 BBC/SWB/ME, 3 August 1990.

4 *The Times*, 8 August 1990.

5 Quoted by the business daily *Dunya* and reproduced in *TPR*, 6 August 1990.

6 BBC/SWB/ME, 8 August 1990.

7 *The Times*, 8 August 1990.

8 *International Herald Tribune*, 8 August 1990.

9 Interview with foreign journalist based in Turkey, 13 November 1990.

10 Other economic benefits were promised by the US including support in the release of $1.4 billion worth of World Bank credits.

11 Other US military promises included the release of 40 used F–4 Phantom fighter–bombers held up since 1984 because of objections by the Greek lobby; an offer to make Eximbank loans available for Turkish military projects (see *The Independent*, 16 August 1990); and a commitment not to reduce US military aid to Turkey of $545 million per annum (*MEI*, no. 385, 12 October 1990).

12 US officials protest that while they remain in favour of Turkey's admission to the EC no promises were made to the Turkish leadership.

13 This belief was also shared by certain foreign journalists based in Turkey, for example Hugh Pope in *The Independent*, 13 August 1990.

14 It is noteworthy that by 12 August there had been four conversations between Presidents Bush and Özal. See *The Independent*, 13 August 1990.

15 A widespread view in Turkey, according to one foreign diplomat, was that if Iraq could use its military power to seize Kuwait's oil resources today then it could use them against Turkey to secure the flow of water in the future (interview, 15 November 1990).

16 Turkish columnist Mehmet Ali Birand, quoted in *The Independent*, 16 August 1990.

17 For example, *Cumhurriyet*, reproduced in *TPR*, 10 August 1990.

18 *Hurriyet*, quoted in *TPR*, 9 August 1990.

19 Interview with *Hurriyet*, quoted in *TPR*, 8 August 1990.

20 Quoted in *TPR*, 8 August 1990.

21 *The Independent*, 4 December 1990.

Chapter 7

1 Ömer Kürkçüoğlu, 'Turkey's attitude towards the Middle East conflict', *Dış Politika* (Foreign Policy), vol. V, no. 4, April 1976, p. 26.

2 Amikam Nachmani, 'Treading the tightrope: Israeli–Turkish relations,

1948–1958', in *Israel, Turkey and Greece* (London: Frank Cass, 1987),
   p. 59.
3 İsmail Soysal, 'Turkish–Arab diplomatic relations after the Second World
   War (1945–1986)', in *Studies on Turkish–Arab Relations* (Istanbul:
   Foundation for Studies on Turkish–Arab Relations, 1986), p. 253.
4 Quoted in ibid.
5 For a discussion of this issue see the appropriate sections in Bülent Ali Rıza,
   'Foreign policy of Turkey toward the Arab states, 1930–1960', unpublished
   doctoral thesis, St Antony's College, Oxford.
6 See Annual Review 1955 produced by British embassy, Ankara, in FO371/
   123999.
7 Nachmani, op. cit., p. 74.
8 Mahmut Bali Aykan, 'Ideology and national interest in Turkish foreign
   policy toward the Muslim world: 1960–87', unpublished doctoral thesis,
   University of Virginia, 1987, p. 79.
9 Kürkçüoğlu, op. cit., p. 31.
10 Nuri Eren, *Turkey Today – And Tomorrow* (London: Pall Mall Press, 1963),
   p. 238.
11 Michael Brecher, *The Foreign Policy System of Israel* (London: Oxford
   University Press, 1972), p. 48.
12 See Michael Bar–Zohar, *Ben–Gurion* (London: Weidenfeld & Nicolson,
   1978), pp. 261–5, for a discussion of the circumstances leading to the
   creation of the pact.
13 Orhan Soysal, 'An analysis of the influences of Turkey's alignment with the
   West and the Arab–Israeli conflict upon Turkish–Israeli and Turkish–Arab
   relations, 1947–77', unpublished doctoral thesis, Princeton University,
   1983, p. 319.
14 Ibid., p. 320.
15 Ferenc A. Vali, *Bridge Across the Bosphorus* (Baltimore, MD: The Johns
   Hopkins Press, 1971), p. 308.
16 Soysal, op. cit., p. 259.
17 The Arab summit in Amman one month before had seen the Palestinian
   question subordinated to the Gulf conflict. For a discussion of the negative
   consequences for the PLO see Lamis Andoni, 'The gains and losses for the
   PLO', *MEI*, no. 313, 21 November 1987.
18 See reports from *Milliyet* and *Cumhurriyet* quoted in *TPR*, 16 May 1990.
19 *Turkey Confidential*, No. 10, June 1990, p. 11.
20 Interview with Zaki Kuneralp, 17 May 1989.
21 Turkey feels a special moral responsibility for the area because it formed
   part of the territory of the Ottoman Empire. However, this rather intangible
   feeling finds little practical expression.
22 According to *TPR*, 22 May 1990, for instance, there was 'general indigna-
   tion' in the Turkish press immediately after the death of seven Palestinians

at the hands of a lone Israeli assassin, and of six as a result of subsequent rioting.

23 Nachmani, op. cit., pp. 54–5.
24 Interview with Tugay Özçeri, 19 October 1989.
25 The community is large and important enough for Israel to deem it worth maintaining a consulate there.
26 Interview with Dr Üzeyir Garih, 11 November 1990.
27 David Hotham, *The Turks* (London: John Murray, 1972), p. 67.
28 Interview with Yehuda Millo, head of Israeli mission to Ankara, *TDN*, 26 July 1990.
29 Ibid.
30 *TPR*, 3 May 1990.
31 See Hugh Pope, 'A 200–ton jellyfish could save the day for thirsty millions', *Wall Street Journal*, 28 May 1990, for more background details.
32 This has been an argument of leading Islamists for some time. For example, see statement by Oğuzhan Asiltürk, Secretary–General of the National Salvation Party, in BBC/SWB/ME, 16 July 1980.

Chapter 8

1 Professor J.A. Allan, *Water Resources in the Middle East: Economic and Strategic Issues* (London: Arab Research Centre Report, October 1989), p. 2.
2 Figure quoted in written presentation by Eng. Zuhair Farah Abu Daud at roundtable discussion on 'The Euphrates Water Issue' convened by Arab Research Centre, London, 19 February 1990.
3 Professor Dr Ali İhsan Bağış, *The Cradle of Civilisation Regenerated* (Istanbul: Gelişim Publishing, 1989), p. 46.
4 Ibid.
5 Abu Daud, op. cit.
6 Allan, op cit.
7 *Syria Country Profile, 1989–90* (London: EIU, 1990), p. 34.
8 Kamran İnan, 'GAP, a project which creates new dimensions in the Middle East', in Erol Manisalı (ed.), *Turkey's Place in the Middle East* (Istanbul: Middle East Business and Banking Publications, 1989), p. 11.
9 Abu Daud, op. cit., during questions at Arab Research Centre symposium.
10 The 'Survey of the Arab world' in *The Economist*, 12 May 1990, p. 10, observes that 'It has become fashionable ... to say that the next war in the Middle East could be fought over water.'
11 Nizar Hamdun, under–secretary in the Iraqi Ministry of Foreign Affairs, led the mission. The content of the proposal was reported by the Associated Press from Baghdad as background information in a dispatch in mid January. See report under headline 'Iraqi aide to rush for talks in Turkey', in

the *Saudi Gazette*, 14 January 1990.

12 'Turkey to Syria and Iraq: "We're sorry but…"', *TDN*, 1 February 1990.

13 See news agency report from Ankara carried in the *Saudi Gazette*, 30 January 1990.

14 Interview with Ankara–based foreign diplomat, 9 May 1990.

15 Abu Daud, op. cit.

16 Quoted in *TDN*, 15 February 1990.

17 Turkish Ministry of Foreign Affairs spokesman Murat Sungar, quoted in *TDN*, 15 February 1990.

18 Fida Nasrallah, 'Middle Eastern waters: the hydraulic imperative', *MEI*, no. 374, 27 April 1990, p. 17.

19 Abu Daud, op. cit.

20 This presumably refers to all those whose livelihood depends directly and indirectly on farming, including the families of farmers and the suppliers of services in those areas.

21 'Survey of the Arab world', *The Economist*, 12 May 1990, p. 12.

22 Much of the detail of Turkey's plans for its 'peace pipeline' is taken from Seyfi Taşhan, 'Water problems in the Middle East and how they could be alleviated', in Manisalı (ed.), op. cit.

Chapter 9

1 For instance, between 1950 and 1960 Turkey's trade volume with the Arab states amounted to between 4 and 5 per cent of total foreign trade. See İsmail Soysal, 'Turkish–Arab diplomatic relations after the Second World War (1945–1986)', in *Studies on Turkish–Arab Relations* (Istanbul: Foundation for Studies on Turkish–Arab Relations, 1986), p. 264.

2 William M. Hale, *The Political and Economic Development of Modern Turkey* (London: Croom Helm, 1981), p. 231.

3 Figures taken from Ali İhsan Bağış, 'The beginning and the development of economic relations between Turkey and Middle Eastern countries', *Diş Politika* (Foreign Policy), vol. XII, nos. 1–2, June 1985, p. 88.

4 Mina Toksoz, *Turkey to 1992: Missing Another Chance?* (London: EIU Special Report No. 1136, 1988), p. 15.

5 See State Institute of Statistics, *Aylik Istatistik Bülteni* (Monthly Bulletin of Statistics) series, published by the Prime Ministry, Ankara.

6 Süha Bölükbaşi, 'Turkey copes with revolutionary Iran', *Journal of South Asian and Middle Eastern Studies*, vol. 13, nos. 1, 2, Fall/Winter 1989, p. 108.

7 These figures only include trade through official channels, ignoring smuggling which is believed to be significant.

8 Bağış, op. cit., p. 92.

9 Oktay Orhon, 'Turkish contracting services abroad', in Erol Manisalı (ed.),

Turkey's Place in the Middle East (Istanbul: Middle East Business and Banking Publications, 1989), p. 89.

10 Ibid., p. 91.

11 Ayfur Barisik, *Turquie 1981* (Paris: OECD, Système d'Observation Permanente des Migrations), table 1, p. 1.

12 Ibid., table 2, p. 2.

13 Ibid., table 6, p. 8.

14 Ayfur Barisik, *Turquie 1986* (Paris: OECD), table 1, p. 1.

15 Figures from *Turizm Istatistikleri 1986* (Ankara: State Institute of Statistics), table 2, p. 5.

16 Ibid., table 12, p. 14.

17 Ibid., table 19, p. 20.

18 International Monetary Fund, *Direction of Trade Statistics Yearbook, 1989* (Washington, DC: IMF, 1989).

19 State Institute of Statistics Monthly Economic Indicators, February 1990.

20 Orhon, op. cit., p. 91.

21 Turkish Contractors Association figures given to author, 14 November 1990.

22 Ibid.

23 BBC/SWB/ME, 17 January 1989.

24 *Financial Times*, 12 December 1988.

25 This had eased to $35.2 billion at the end of 1989. See *Turkey on Trial* (London: EIU, 1989), p. 35.

26 *Financial Times*, 11 August 1989.

27 *Iraq* (London: Business International Global Forecasting Service, first quarter 1990), p. 25.

28 *Turkey Confidential*, No. 7, March 1990, p. 5.

29 For example, see *Newspot*, 17 April 1990.

CHATHAM HOUSE PAPERS

Also in this series

India's Foreign Policy since 1971
Robert W. Bradnock

The author analyses the impact of domestic political and economic changes on foreign policy since 1971, when Indian regional dominance was confirmed by the break-up of Pakistan. The study looks at India's complex relationships both with its immediate neighbours and with the superpowers, and tries to assess its future role in the wider international scene.   Publication: September 1990

East Central Europe
from Reform to Transformation
Judy Batt

This book provides a concise account of the breakdown of communist rule in Poland, Hungary and Czechoslovakia and a comparative analysis of the problems and prospects of their transition to pluralist democratic politics and market economies. A major theme is the linkage of politics and economics: the book shows how both the failure of economic reforms in Poland and Hungary, and the resistance to economic reform, contributed to undermining the communist monopoly of power; and how the new politics of multi-party pluralism interact with the unprecedented task of radical economic transformation.   Publication: June 1991

Remaking the Balkans
Christopher Cviic

This is the first English publication to analyse the political and security implications for South-Eastern Europe of the collapse of communism. For more than four decades, the cold war had ensured not only a flow of aid into the region but also a certain kind of stability. Now that it is no longer of strategic importance whether any countries in the region change allegiance, the old disputes between them have assumed a more important role. This study suggests how various mechanisms could be used to contain the crisis in the short term.   Publication: July 1991

RIIA/PINTER PUBLISHERS